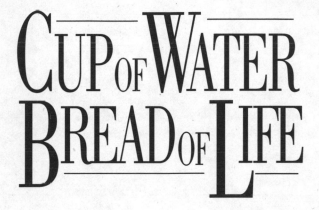

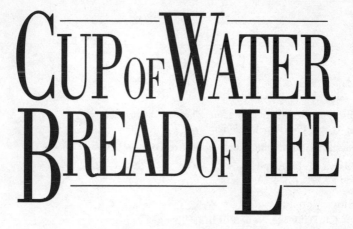

CUP OF WATER BREAD OF LIFE

INSPIRING STORIES ABOUT OVERCOMING LOPSIDED CHRISTIANITY

RONALD J. SIDER

ZondervanPublishingHouse
Grand Rapids, Michigan

A Division of HarperCollinsPublishers

Cup of Water, Bread of Life
Inspiring Stories About Overcoming Lopsided Christianity
Copyright © 1994 Ronald J. Sider

Requests for information should be addressed to:

Zondervan Publishing House
Grand Rapids, MI 49530

    Sider, Ronald J.
      Cup of water, bread of life / Ronald J. Sider.
        p. cm.
      Includes bibliographical references.
      ISBN 0-310-40601-3 (alk. paper)
      1. Evangelistic work. 2. Church and social problems. 3. Church
    renewal. I. Title.
    BV3790.S548 1994   94-26605
    261.8′3—dc20   CIP

Edited by Mary McCormick
Cover design by John M. Lucas

Printed in the United States of America

94 95 96 97 98 99 00 01 02 03 / ❖ DH / 10 9 8 7 6 5 4 3 2

This edition is printed on acid-free paper and meets the American National Standards Institute Z39.48 standard.

To:
John and Vera Mae Perkins

Contents

Acknowledgments

John and Vera Mae Perkins, to whom this book is dedicated, have been teachers and mentors on wholistic development for thousands around the world. We love and appreciate them and thank God for sharing them with us.

I am very grateful to all the wonderful people whose stories are shared here. For their dedication, witness, and the time they generously gave to make this book possible I want to say a deeply felt thank-you.

Several gifted colleagues helped make this book possible. Donald Fitzkee traveled around the world interviewing people and gathering the data I used to write this book. Without his careful research, this book would not have been written. Robertoluis Lugo discovered the puzzling world of my hasty handwriting as he patiently and carefully typed the manuscript. My graduate assistant, Heidi Rolland, did painstaking proofreading and careful research for Chapter 10 on abominably short notice. And Naomi Miller, my administrative secretary, brought her superb skills and gentle patience to the usual time of final madness connected with completing manuscripts for the publisher's deadline. Thank you, good friends.

Introduction

"Don't tell me what to do, show me *how*." If that is how you feel, read on.

I meet numerous Christians who truly believe that Jesus—not some one-sided caricature, to be sure, but the full-blooded biblical Christ—is truly the answer to today's toughest problems. I meet many Christians who genuinely want to combine evangelism and social concern, and they long to share Christ's love with the whole person in an honest, effective way. But they are not sure *how*. "Give me an example," people often say after I finish my theological plea to overcome one-sided Christianity. That is why I wrote this book of stories.

I used to sell *World Book Encyclopedia*s to pay my way through college. One of the best sales lines was: "A picture is worth a thousand words." This book is full of pictures—extended pictures of ten of the best wholistic ministries from around the world, and scores of little snapshots of many, many ordinary people serving and being served.

This book is a companion volume to *One-Sided Christianity? Uniting the Church to Heal a Lost and Broken World*. In that earlier book, I described the biblical foundations for integrating evangelism and social transformation in the power of the Spirit. That book tells the stories of people who are doing that. Together the two books provide the theory and practice of wholistic mission.

This is a book of stories, not a "how-to" manual. But the "how-to"s are here even though they are not presented by abstract, theoretical analysis. These stories share the pilgrimages of some of today's most effective Christian church leaders and successful programs in wholistic mission. As I studied and wrote about their journeys and programs, new practical ideas for my own work kept popping into my head. I am sure the same will happen for you.

Two warnings are important. Don't glorify the people in these stories as superheroes. And don't overlook their failures.

I wanted to tell stories, so I had to talk about specific people.

Some of them protested, insisting that they are just ordinary, struggling pilgrims like everyone else. They rightly reminded me that their ministry was possible only because scores and scores of faithful colleagues have journeyed with them, sharing the agony, disappointment, hard work, and joy. All of that is true and important. Around each major story, I have woven subplots about some of these faithful partners and the people they serve. But there is not space to tell everyone's story, so I have chosen—knowing all the limitations of this approach—to weave the story around the central person or couple in each example.

Every ministry has failures. You will see in the following pages how even the most successful programs grow out of and frequently experience disappointment, opposition, mistakes, and failure.

Lest these stories discourage those who have toiled and cried and never seen the kind of dramatic success presented here, I want to confess my own personal failure. For more than a decade, my wife, Arbutus, and I worked as hard as we knew how to develop the kind of wholistic ministry this book describes. John Perkins' interracial vision and wholistic integration of evangelism and social concern were our inspiration as we worked with others in a desperately poor part of inner-city Philadelphia. But our job-creation program failed. Personalities clashed. Some community people fought our Christ-centered approach. Eventually the congregation explicitly abandoned the interracial, wholistic vision. We cried, grieved—and were tremendously strengthened by the fact that good friends like the ones in these stories have been far more successful in other places.

Applying Jesus' healing balm to all the needs of real persons is the only way to be faithful to our Lord. But it is not easy. If you have tried and failed, I understand your pain. My prayer is that the stories here will give you the energy and hope to try again.

I have absolutely no doubt whatsoever that if ten percent of the Christians in the world today would obey Jesus' commission in John 20:21, we would experience explosive church growth and sweeping social transformation. "As the Father has sent me, I am sending you," Jesus commanded. Our Lord cared about the whole person in community, and so should we. When we share the whole Gospel with the whole person, God works miracles in the lives of the poor, broken, and hopeless. Individuals are remade, and societies are transformed.

More and more Christians agree on the theory. But how do we do it? It's in the practical area that we need help. Reading the stories of those who have created effective wholistic ministries is one of the best ways to learn how to do it ourselves.

The ten fantastic stories in this book demonstrate that wholistic ministry works. They show that using Jesus' approach is not just right but also practical.

Caring for the whole person, to be sure, is costly and challenging. But it is far from impossible. As I travel around the world, I meet more and more people whom God is using in dramatic ways to transform persons and communities. Jesus' whole Gospel is the most powerful message the world has ever seen and heard.

1
Fighting Apartheid and Evangelizing the Oppressed; Caesar Molebatsi and Youth Alive

I refuse to let any man belittle my soul by making me hate him.

Booker T. Washington

Caesar Molebatsi is a black South African who has every reason to hate whites. A white man purposely smashed his car into Caesar one day when as a fifteen-year-old he was out riding on his bicycle. Caesar lost one of his legs—in fact, he almost died. Bitterness burned within him and his passion for revenge threatened to destroy him. But the love of Christ conquered his anger and transformed his life.

Today Caesar leads Youth Alive Ministries based in Soweto, South Africa. It is one of the most successful evangelistic and black leadership training organizations in the whole country. Over the past thirty years, thirty thousand young people have been members of Youth Alive. The vast majority had become Christians by the time they graduated.

Caesar's personal story mirrors both the tragedy and the promise of multi-racial South Africa. As a boy he loved to visit the lovely farming village of Boons where his grandfather's family had lived and owned land for over eighty years. In the early 1960s, however, the white apartheid government declared Boons a white area. When the blacks refused to move, the government bulldozed the school and the church, destroyed the water supply, and threatened to destroy all the homes. Reluctantly, the villagers agreed to move to a black homeland. They never received a cent for their property.

Until the legal structures of apartheid were abolished in the early 1990s, blacks (75 percent of the population) could only own land in homelands that covered only thirteen percent of South Africa. The white minority (about fourteen percent) owned the other eighty-seven percent. Ruthless police tactics enabled the white minority to enjoy most of the wealth and exclude blacks from voting.

In spite of the white racism, Caesar's father hoped that education offered a way forward for black South Africans. He worked as a teacher in the large school system operated for blacks by the Anglican church. But in 1955, the apartheid government passed the Bantu Education Act, which took over these church schools. Why? To make sure the education offered blacks was "appropriate" to their inferior position in society.

Caesar's dad had been an active Anglican and a Sunday school superintendent, but when the church failed to protest the new racist educational law, he left the church, angry and disillusioned. He taught his children to reject organized Christianity that failed to take a stand against racism.

The white driver who almost killed Caesar the day before Christmas 1964 was a typical product of that racism. As Caesar rode his bicycle along the road near his home, a white man, driving too fast, started to pass Caesar at a curve. Suddenly another car rounded the curve coming from the other direction. The first car still had time to break to stay behind the black boy on the bicycle until the other car had passed. Instead he continued at high speed. Too late, the white driver realized that he risked a head-on collision with the other car—unless he purposely smashed into the little black boy on the bicycle. He yanked the steering wheel. Caesar's body went flying, a tangled mass of broken bones and bent bicycle parts.

The white driver was never punished. Caesar's dad tried to take him to court, but the (white) police accepted the (white) driver's lie that Caesar had been drunk. When his dad tried again, the policeman dismissed him, suggesting that blacks were "lazy animals."

Caesar plotted revenge. He hated all whites, especially that white driver. With his brother, George, he made plans to burn down the man's home.

God had other plans. Caesar was a successful biology student in high school, and a militant anti-Christian. One day a speaker from a Christian youth movement called Youth Alive came to address his student assembly on Jesus' resurrection. Fellow students expected Caesar to lead the attack. Caesar was ready with his best "contradictions in the Bible" speech. But his hot words of ridicule froze in his mouth as he listened. A few weeks later he attended another Youth Alive meeting. He was impressed by the sincere, devout young Christians he met.

The presence of one white couple, however, almost pushed him away. He had absolutely no trust in white people or white religion, but the obvious love for Christ of the young black Christians in Youth Alive moved him to reconsider. The more he got involved with Youth Alive's programs, the more he felt drawn to Christ, although he still struggled with his political ambitions and his hatred. At that time Caesar says, "I saw myself as an articulate educated activist. . . . In my mind, political legislation was the only way to bring about change."[1]

During a Youth Alive retreat in April 1967, Caesar fought and struggled with his decision. Could he really come to love the white people he deeply hated? Finally, the last night of the retreat, Caesar said yes. He resolved to follow Christ no matter what the cost.

A short time later, before most students knew he had turned from his former hostility, Caesar unexpectedly received an opportunity to speak to all the twelve hundred students in his high school. Trembling, he told them how a white man had crippled him for life and how he had rejected Christianity as a white man's religion. Then he explained his new discovery that organized religion was quite different from a personal encounter with Jesus Christ.

His life ministry as an evangelist began at that moment. More than fourteen students came forward to ask what had happened to him, and several became Christians that day.

Caesar threw himself into the work of Youth Alive, quickly becoming a leader. In one three-month period he and other Christian high school students visited every high school in

Soweto, the largest black "township" —i.e., city—in South Africa. They spoke to thousands in large assemblies, and scores came to Christ. Caesar had planned to become a lawyer, but now he felt a growing call to preach and evangelize. He gladly accepted the invitation from Youth Alive leaders to travel all across South Africa as part of a young evangelistic team. Stunning success led to opportunities to tour England and the United States.

A devout businessman whom he met in New Jersey eventually made it possible for him to study first as an undergraduate at Northeastern Bible College and then as a graduate student at Wheaton College. After graduation in June 1976, Caesar and his wife, Chumi, planned to travel across the United States. They hoped to enlist people to support them with prayer and money when they returned to South Africa.

Two days later Soweto exploded. Police killed black Soweto high-school students who were protesting the white Afrikaner government's demand that subjects like science and math be taught in Afrikaans. Thousands marched and hundreds died. South Africa's black high-school students had seized the initiative. Their action precipitated events that would lead eventually to the end of apartheid, but much struggle and bloodshed would come first.

Caesar and Chumi rushed back to Soweto, where they found Youth Alive ready for new black leadership. Allen Lutz, the white missionary who cofounded and then led Youth Alive from 1960–1976, insisted that white missionaries should no longer lead or control Youth Alive. To the white, conservative missionary organization for which Allen had worked, that was outrageous. Like most other missionary organizations in South Africa, Caesar says, they still "held on to the old-fashioned racist view that black people could not run organizations by themselves." So Allen Lutz left, Youth Alive broke with the missions agency, and Caesar became the new Executive Director.

Caesar changed the name to Youth Alive Ministries to underline his intention to be more wholistic. Evangelism was still central, but the youth were encouraged to debate politics and justice. Soweto's youth, caught up in the swirling excitement of the rebellion against apartheid, loved it.

White missionaries, however, did not. Nor did the conservative black pastors they had trained. White missionaries had taught that Christians should ignore politics and concentrate on saving souls. When Youth Alive Ministries (YAM) challenged the government's racist policies and demanded justice, some white missionaries called Caesar and his black colleagues "Communists." Fortunately, YAM was independent. Even though they lost support, YAM insisted on doing both evangelism and social action.

The result has been an organization that has led thousands and thousands of black South Africans to Jesus Christ and trained them to become articulate leaders. This would never have been possible if YAM had been under white control. The wholistic message of vital, dynamic personal faith in Jesus Christ that was constantly related to the social, economic, and political needs of blacks living under apartheid was powerful and relevant. Thousands flocked to YAM clubs, retreats, and assemblies.

When my wife, Arbutus, and I visited South Africa in early 1993, we were amazed at the ways in which we kept meeting and learning about prominent black South African professionals and other leaders who had been discipled by YAM. They are everywhere—pastors, doctors, lawyers, dentists, teachers, scientists, engineers. The most prominent include Cyril Ramaphosa, a lawyer and former chair of the board of Youth Alive. Ramaphosa is now General Secretary of the African National Congress and chairs the group writing South Africa's new constitution.

What is it in YAM's youth programs that develops this kind of strong, vigorous Christian leadership? I learned part of the answer when I talked with Abe Matlou, regional director of YAM for Soweto.

Abe attended Soweto's Morris Isaacson High School, which led the June 1976 Uprising. The key leadership came from his class. Abe was there when the first plans were made. Marches, police brutality, and scores of deaths quickly followed. Normal schooling ended in Soweto for all of 1976.

Abe and two of his friends made plans to blow up a bridge. One of the friends stole explosives from the mine where he worked and Abe hid them in a bag in the ground. Their plan was disrupted when a rainstorm destroyed the explosives.

Soon after that disappointment, Abe attended his first Youth Alive rally. In spite of regular church attendance, he had never heard the Gospel clearly presented the way it was that night as young, black high-school students sang and shared their testimonies. Two weeks later, he accepted Christ.

It was Youth Alive (which he joined three weeks after his conversion) that discipled Abe. "I knew nothing about leadership," Abe confesses. But at his first YAM meeting, he was asked to read the Scriptures. Three months later, Abe was chosen to be a leader in one of the clubs. (Annually every YAM club elects a president, vice-president, secretary, treasurer, and transportation coordinator. Before the elections, club leaders provide teaching about the qualities of leadership, the responsibility of voting, and the principles of democracy.) Abe didn't have much biblical knowledge. But he learned quickly from the leadership training and biblical instruction offered by his club's co-sponsors (more mature senior high-school students appointed by YAM staff) and sponsor (a young adult appointed by YAM to provide overall direction and guidance to the club). A year later Abe was appointed a co-sponsor. By his third year he ran an annual camp for more than one hundred students. He was learning fast.

Maximum participation by every person is one of YAM's guiding principles for leadership training. It certainly worked in Abe's case. Today he directs about four hundred-fifty Youth Alivers in nine different clubs in Soweto, helping kids grow in Christ in the same way he was helped.

Abe explained the way YAM works with each person. When students join YAM, they receive an initial three-week orientation to YAM's mission. They are invited to accept Christ but are welcomed into a club even if they do not. Then they join a club, and that club's leader receives a written statement of where that person is at spiritually. Once in the club, every person has some responsibility, but only Christians lead the spiritual parts of the program. YAM's quiz teams compete at quiz festivals that deal with both the Bible and current economic and political affairs. YAM also sponsors sports festivals. And they encourage vigorous debate about everything from sexuality and dating to the political future of the country. YAM deals with the whole person.

Abe explained how evangelism happens in YAM programs. Much evangelism occurs in the local YAM club (twenty to fifty members). Every weekly program includes a personal challenge. Once a month every club member invites four non-Christian friends to a special meeting, where the Gospel is presented and youth are invited to accept Christ. Personal, one-to-one evangelism is also encouraged. Team leaders train every member in personal evangelism and encourage each person to share his or her faith. A couple times a year several clubs together sponsor a large public event featuring music or drama. Each club member invites non-Christians. Special speakers with unusual gifts for communicating with young people share the Gospel. Annual camps and retreats like the one where Caesar finally yielded to Christ offer a fourth major avenue for evangelism. YAM has a powerful, effective evangelistic ministry.

My talk with Molefi Mataboge demonstrated how YAM's wholistic evangelistic approach works. By the time Molefi first attended a YAM meeting in 1985, he was a very sophisticated political leader in his high school. He was vice-chair of the Student Representative Council for his high school and a member of the Soweto Student Congress, so he had to take extraordinary steps to avoid being arrested by the police. During the day while at school, he was relatively safe since the Afrikaner principal of his high school would have been in danger if the police had arrested such a prominent student leader at school. So the police struck at night, between 1:00 and 2:00 A.M.. From 1984–1986 Molefi often stayed at friends' houses until 3:00 A.M.., returning home after that when the danger of police arrest was less. That meant just three or four hours of sleep.

Neither Molefi nor his parents were Christians when he first accepted a YAM member's invitation to attend a YAM meeting in March, 1985. The first thing this young student activist did was to check out YAM's interest in socio-political issues. YAM passed that test! The other thing that attracted him powerfully was the different lifestyle of YAM members. Molefi had become disappointed with the liquor and sex that seemed so much a part of student politics. At YAM he saw young people who were politically engaged, yet different. At a YAM rally in 1985 the speaker helped Molefi see that being a Christian meant committing one-self personally to Christ. Molefi took the plunge.

Now Molefi found a new challenge. He struggled to relate his new faith in Christ to his ongoing political work as vice-chair of the Student Representative Council. Fortunately, YAM was running programs that dealt with the Christian's response to politics. When he asked Abe Matlou, the sponsor of his YAM club, whether his political work was appropriate, Abe encouraged him to continue. "Just don't do anything that contradicts Christ," Abe added.

Soweto high schools in the mid- to late 1980s were full of chaos, disruptions, strikes, and violence. Final exams were not possible in either 1985 or 1986. One day the whole student body sang boisterous songs to prevent the principal from addressing the assembly. In desperation the principal asked Molefi to speak to the student body. When Molefi asked them to go to class, they did. On the way to class, however, a soldier used his rifle to beat a student for walking too slowly. Angrily, several students attacked the soldiers, who called for help. The soldiers shot and killed one student. When the principal (wrongly) blamed Molefi, it became too dangerous for him to attend school. He continued to function as vice-chair but did his studies at the YAM center rather than at his high school.

Molefi is an effective evangelist. He joined one of YAM's Gospel Teams that give each member special training in evangelism. Gospel Teams use drama, music, and preaching to present the Gospel. When I asked Molefi in March 1993 how many people he had led to Christ, he said, "A lot more than fifty!" Molefi is only twenty-five years old.

Since 1989 Molefi has been a part-time volunteer with YAM. He has also studied mechanical engineering. He hopes to work full-time at YAM soon.

YAM has obviously changed Molefi's life. "When YAM looked at me," he told me, "they did not just see a soul; instead they saw a person with needs. They dealt with my whole being. They helped me grow in all spheres: physical, social, and spiritual." Molefi told me that people outside YAM sometimes ask in amazement why YAM members are so confident. Molefi has an answer: "At YAM you learn to ask questions. You debate."

YAM today has clubs not only in Soweto but also in Capetown, Zululand, and in the neighboring country of Zimbabwe. Every week YAM ministers to about 1,500 youths. Everywhere YAM's goal is "to reach out and minister to young people with a relevant, holistic development programme that nurtures, sustains and motivates them to become Christians for transformation in church and society."

We have already seen how YAM implements this wholistic mission through vigorous evangelism and leadership training. Community development is also part of YAM's work: the education support program; the feeding and relief program; the women's development program; the twilight program; and the small-business development program. In all its development work, however, YAM works with the philosophy that community development is not primarily about services like health care or education. Rather, "it has to do with people, people's education, organisation, and their discipline. Transformation of a community is possible with changed people, and the Gospel of Christ enables people to change fundamentally, and impact their society."[2]

The education-support program offers extra tutoring on evenings and weekends for students in government schools. Apartheid policies plus the massive unrest in the schools have created a monumental educational crisis. In 1993, classes averaged sixty students per teacher. Only ten percent of black students entering primary school reached the last year of high school, and only one-third of those passed their final exams! YAM's education-support program uses qualified volunteer teachers to provide specialized tutoring so that more young people can receive a good education.

The feeding-and-relief program has provided food to very poor families. The women's development program, run in Soweto by Caesar's wife, Chumi, offers health and nutrition lectures, and a sewing program to teach poor women how to sew and market their products. Chumi also hopes to develop a women's cooperative that will buy food cheaply in bulk and then enable women to resell what they do not need at a reasonable profit.

The twilight program seeks to minister to the thousands of

street children in places like Soweto. They need food, love, and education.

I talked to Mahlomola Sithole. His parents divorced in 1978. Since then he has struggled, sometimes living with his grandmother, sometimes living in the streets. Mahlomola first came into contact with YAM through one of their soup kitchens after his grandmother died in 1982. In 1986 he became a Christian through YAM and began to participate in their twilight program. Since 1991 he has lived at the YAM center in Soweto.

Mahlomola told me that most of the people he grew up with are on drugs or trapped by alcoholism or in jail. YAM helped him avoid those tragedies.

YAM's most ambitious development program, called Joshua Projects, is still largely in the planning stage. The goal of the Joshua Projects is to develop medium-sized businesses in places like Soweto. By providing capital and business training for gifted entrepreneurs, the program hopes to help develop businesses that will provide jobs and create a new economic base for both families and the Youth Alive Ministries.

If directing YAM were all that Caesar Molebatsi did, his life and work would be a significant contribution to the twentieth-century church. But Caesar's work goes far beyond YAM. He has played a significant role in the church's struggle against apartheid, helped found several new organizations, planted a new church, and been active in the worldwide evangelical movement.

Caesar has been actively engaged in the major church-based initiatives—the Kairos document, the National Initiative on Reconciliation, and the Rustenberg Declaration—to end apartheid. Again and again he was frustrated and hurt as evangelicals, especially white evangelicals, questioned his biblical commitments because of his political engagement. Eventually Caesar and some other black evangelical leaders formed a new organization, Concerned Evangelicals (CE), to help develop a thoroughly biblical, vigorously activist response to the unjust situation in South Aftica.

Caesar co-edited CE's first publication, *Evangelical Witness in South Africa* (1986).[3] It is a ringing call to reject the kind of one-sided Christianity that ignored or even quietly supported apartheid while emphasizing that the church's task was evange-lism, not socio-economic liberation. *Evangelical Witness* denounced that approach as a tool of oppression. It summoned "all committed evangelicals in South Africa to come out boldly to be witnesses of the gospel of salvation, justice and peace. . . . If we fail now, we shall have no legitimacy in the post-liberation period."[4]

As chair of the board, Caesar helped develop CE into a rally-ing place for black evangelicals who wanted to join the political struggle for justice without abandoning their passion for evange-lism or their commitment to biblical theology. Through its regu-lar publication, conferences on socio-political issues, and direct engagement in the struggle against apartheid, CE has exercised significant impact.

One of CE's more ambitious projects has been the Evangelical Theological House of Studies (ETHOS) located at the University of Natal in Pietermaritzburg. ETHOS provides a place where black evangelicals can do their theological training in a setting that seeks to be both deeply biblical and contextually relevant. Unlike so many of the white-led, missionary-controlled evangel-ical centers for theological training, ETHOS dares to grapple vig-orously with socio-political questions. It seeks to develop a black theology that is also thoroughly evangelical.

After ministering for a number of years in a church controlled by white missionaries, Caesar and a small circle of friends formed Ebenezer Evangelical Church in 1982. Carefully they prepared a constitution that reflected their eagerness, in Caesar's words, "to maintain a balance between preaching the Gospel of God's grace and speaking out on sociopolitical conditions."[5] Meeting first in a garage and then in a school classroom, the congregation grew. In 1990 one hundred-fifty rejoicing people dedicated their first church building. In spite of his hectic schedule, Caesar finds time to serve as pastor of Ebenezer Evangelical Church.

Many other things make heavy demands on Caesar's time. He serves as president of the YMCA for South Africa. He is a member of the Theological Commission of the World Evangelical Fellowship and gave a plenary address at the Lausanne Committee for World Evangelization's Manila assembly. He is active in the African branch of the International Fellowship of

Evangelical Missions Theologians. In 1993, he agreed to chair an interracial, South African committee working with David Bussau (see chapter seven) to make loans to small black entrepreneurs so they can start new businesses.

Along with all this national and international work, Caesar found time to serve on the Regional and Local Dispute Resolution Committees of the National Peace Accords in the early '90s. Violence and massacre, motivated by ethnic and political tensions, constantly threatened to undermine the transition to a truly democratic, multi-racial society. Regularly, at almost any time of the day or night, Caesar could be called to the gruesome scenes of death to document the evil and to discourage further violence.

Soweto is not a safe, comfortable place to live and raise a family. Raging unemployment and poverty encourage widespread crime. An incident that occurred while I was visiting South Africa in March 1993 is not unusual. During the middle of the day three men came to the home of one of Caesar's colleagues in YAM and asked to speak to him. When he stepped outside to talk, they pointed a gun at him. "We don't want to kill you," they assured him. "Just give us the keys to the minibus." Nobody got hurt that time, but YAM's programs suffered disruption because of the stolen vehicle. And the psychological pressure under which Caesar and his colleagues must constantly work shot up another couple of degrees.

The long struggle against white oppression has taken its toll. Caesar works gladly in partnership with people of all races to build a new South Africa that will be open and just for all. But he can never forget what happened to that young fifteen-year-old riding his bicycle around a curve in the road. The temptation of bitterness, hatred, and revenge is still what he fears the most. "I have to pray daily," he confesses, "God, please save me today from bitterness. Save me today from irrational hatred."[6]

In spite of danger and ongoing struggle, Caesar is hopeful. With cautious optimism he looks ahead to a new South Africa where all can share the land's abundance. And he believes deeply that the kind of wholistic ministry God has led him to develop is exactly what is needed. "As long as I live, I want nothing more than to see the church of Jesus Christ in South Africa rise triumphantly from the ashes of colonialism and the bankruptcy of apartheid to proclaim the living Lord who saves people from their sins and from the shackles of poverty, injustice, and racism."[7]

1 Ceasar Molebatsi, *A Flame for Justice*. (Oxford: Lion Paperback, 1991), 59. This chapter is based on personal interviews plus this book by Molebatsi.

2 From YAM flier.

3 Outside South Africa, it was published first in *Transformation*, January-March 1987, 17–30. Later it was published in the U.S. by Eerdmans with a foreword by Dr. Deotis Roberts.

4 Quoted in Molebatsi, *Flame for Justice*, 137.

5 Ibid., 149.

6 Ibid., 92.

7 Ibid., 155.

2

Words, Works, and Wonders Among the Poor of London

From the very beginning, I thought that whatever God calls me to do,
I need to be in a place where I can serve the poor.

Roger Foster

I sat rapt with attention as Faith Forster told me about her fifteen-year-old son dying of cancer. In early 1982, Chris Forster had been healthy and full of life. Then breathlessness and chest pains prompted a chest X-ray. To everyone's astonishment, doctors discovered cancer all over his chest. More tests showed rapidly growing cancer all through his lymphatic system, and even worse, in his spinal fluid. Doctors held out virtually no hope at all. They gave Chris only a few months to live.

Filled with grief, Faith and her husband Roger asked their entire church to pray with them. Already in 1982, Ichthus Fellowship was unusual. It was growing rapidly because of extensive work in both evangelism and social outreach. It was both evangelical and charismatic, both politically engaged and a center of intercessory prayer and spiritual warfare. Ichthus also believed in divine healing. For seven years they had been praying for the sick, with only occasional healings. But everyone prayed fervently for Chris. On the first Wednesday after he entered the hospital, the whole congregation fasted and prayed.

That same Wednesday, a Canadian stranger connected with Youth With a Mission showed up to pray with them. At the hospital, Faith, Roger, and the stranger prayed mightily for Chris's healing. In fact, they prayed so loudly that Chris's doctor heard them as he attended other patients nearby! Faith told me that she felt God's presence in a very powerful way as they prayed that day. She left the hospital, fully convinced that God was healing Chris.

The next day, Chris looked entirely different. Pain, cough, and breathlessness were all gone. When they X-rayed Chris the following Monday, his chest was entirely clear. Two days later, they tested his spinal fluid. Again, there was no sign whatsoever of the cancer that had been everywhere just a week earlier.

The doctors could not understand. After a long review of the medical data some time later, one of the doctors admitted to Faith that he simply had no explanation. He even confessed that he quite understood why she believed that God had miraculously healed Chris!

Today, eleven years later, Chris is a healthy, happy husband active in Ichthus Fellowship. My conversation with him was inspiring. He loves to tell the story of God's astounding gift to him.

Chris's healing encouraged the entire fellowship. Ichthus did not abandon its focus on evangelism and social concern. But healing and the other charismatic gifts became more central in its life.

Today, Ichthus Fellowship is a body with an average weekly attendance of about two thousand adults and seven hundred children worshiping in about thirty congregations in London. Starting in 1974 with fourteen people in a working-class district of southeast London, Ichthus grew rapidly because of its unusual combination of evangelism and ministry to the needy. Many of its members are converts drawn to the church by its social compassion. In inner-city London, average church attendance is about 10.7 percent (and evangelical church attendance is a mere 3.9 percent.) But in the inner-city borough of Lewisham where Ichthus has been working for almost twenty years, church attendance is fifteen percent. (And evangelical church attendance is 9.6 percent!) Today Ichthus's impact reaches around the world—through its extensive foreign missionary work, books and speeches by its leaders, the music of Ichthus's worship leader Graham Kendrick, and the Marches for Jesus that started as local events at Ichthus.[1]

Many different people have prayed and struggled together to make Ichthus what it is today. Without literally scores of committed, gifted leaders, it would not exist or continue. But space does not allow me to tell you about all of those dedicated folk. Instead I will share the pilgrimages of Roger and Faith Forster, the leaders of the original core of folk who launched Ichthus twenty years ago.

Roger came to Christ through the Christian Union (called IVCF in North America) while studying mathematics at Cambridge, one of England's oldest, most prestigious universities. In the liberal Methodist tradition of his childhood, he never heard a clear message of sin, forgiveness, and eternal life, but one night at the Christian Union, an Anglican bishop explained the Gospel in a way that overwhelmed Roger with God's love. On the way home, he quietly gave his life to Christ.

Soon he was going to every possible meeting in the Christian Union—prayer meetings, lectures, visits to hospitals, and prisons. "I was just hungry to know God." He wandered around Cambridge with a Bible in one pocket and Thomas à Kempis in the other.

One day while reading a book attacking Christianity, he unexpectedly experienced God's loving presence in a most dramatic way. The book quoted Peter's words to the Lord, "Lord, you know that I love you." As Roger read these words, a river of love suddenly poured through the room. It felt, Roger says, like "sine curves of love going through the room, going through the chairs, and through the table legs and through me. I shut my eyes and put my hands out and I touched God. I just wept. It was sweet, so sweet and intense, that God loved me. I was just talking to God out loud because he was just there." It only lasted for three days, but that was long enough for some (Christian) friends to think he had gone mad. And long enough to leave an indelible mark on the rest of his life.

The person at the Christian Union's book table informed Roger that if he wanted to be a good evangelical he must read the two volumes of Hudson Taylor, the famous missionary to China. He did. Zeal to spread the Gospel everywhere has been a passionate concern ever since.

Already at Cambridge, the key elements of Roger's lifelong ministry were taking shape. His evangelistic passion was powerful. In spite of his elite Cambridge education, he also was deeply concerned for the poor. "From the very beginning I thought that whatever God calls me to do, I need to be in a place where I can serve the poor and abandon privilege." With increasing longing, Roger also searched for a church that transcended narrow denominationalism and experienced genuine community and body life. All the churches he saw seemed to be "lots of individuals trying to do things together rather than enjoying a corporate body experience." Later, when he studied the Reformation and learned about the Anabaptists, he found the kind of Christian community for which he was searching. Evangelism intertwined with social concern, biblical fidelity, the church as community, and the guiding, empowering presence of the Holy Spirit—these were to be Roger's central, lifelong concerns.

After graduation from Cambridge, Roger served as an officer in the Royal Air Force, but his major preoccupation was evangelizing fellow soldiers! He led a growing congregation on the military base and preached the Gospel everywhere, even over the public-address system. (When the chaplain objected, Roger won permission from the commanding officer!) Revival struck. They sold one hundred-sixty big Bibles in one six-week period. The camp's whole atmosphere changed. Roger took many of the new converts to surrounding churches. When he left the Air Force, those churches asked him to help them with preaching and teaching.

During these same years, God was developing a similar vision in the heart of Faith. Faith went to church with her uncle. At four, she accepted Christ. "As young as I can possibly remember, I was committing my life to Jesus Christ," Faith says. "He was the most wonderful person I had ever heard about." At about age thirteen, Faith felt a clear call to serve Christ in some special way. When this young teenager of thirteen explained that to her minister, he began to encourage and teach her. She did evangelism and led the youth group. When the minister went on holidays when Faith was seventeen, he asked her to lead the church's midweek Bible study. Because of her minister's encouragement, it never crossed Faith's mind at the time that some might consider this activity inappropriate for a woman.

About the same time, Faith sensed a new hunger for the Holy Spirit. In a neighboring Pentecostal Church, she sought and found the "baptism of the Holy Spirit."

As she devoured missionary biographies, Faith determined to be a foreign missionary. To do that, she needed a practical skill. So at seventeen, she left her study of English literature and turned to nursing. Working with the Wycliffe Bible Translators, she prepared for missions abroad.

Then she met Roger. Fortunately he, too, planned to go as a foreign missionary. Roger, however, had a strange idea. He thought that before he went to evangelize in other lands, he first ought to demonstrate that the church can reach those in need at home. At that time in the mid-sixties, there was very little social concern in evangelical churches. But social passion burned strong in Roger's heart. As they dated and prepared for marriage, Roger and Faith dreamed of ministering to London's tramps, drug addicts, and other social rejects neglected by Christians.

So what do you think they did with the money given them as a wedding present? Right after their marriage (in 1965), they used it to buy a big, old, run-down house in Kent near London where they could minister to society's rejects. The homeless, the poor, the mentally disturbed—all came, and they all were welcomed. Surrounding churches were more than happy to get rid of their truly problematic people. Gladly, they sent them to Roger and Faith. At 2:00 A.M. one morning, the local policeman knocked. Could the homeless woman he had just arrested and would otherwise lock up in jail stay with them? They agreed. For three and a half years they ministered to all who came—cooking, cleaning, feeding, and nurturing. They saw persons saved, demons cast out, and people healed.

Slowly, however, Faith became exhausted. Roger was often traveling as a successful evangelist holding missions in churches and universities. Their two little babies demanded time. So they finally sold the house and moved back to southeast London where Roger had grown up.

Roger continued his evangelistic work, but his heart was restless. The many conversions delighted him, but he longed to be able to help disciple those new Christians and join a team building a genuine Christian community.

The opportunity came in 1974. That year the Evangelical Alliance of Britain sponsored a national evangelistic campaign for local churches called Power Project. Roger and his full-time evangelistic colleague Roger Mitchell, led the local effort in London's Peckham District and the surrounding area. This area's population was largely working class, although some middle-class folk live there. But many residents lived in drug-infested, crime ridden, government-owned, high-rise apartment buildings ("council estate?"). There seemed to be no home for the new converts from the council estates. Finally Roger and Faith were asked to start a new congregation, with evangelism as the central focus. Roger visited the other churches, asking if anyone objected to his planting a new church among the folk from the council estates. Much relieved, every single minister gladly agreed!

In September 1974, about fourteen people started a fellowship in Forest Hill that was to grow in less than twenty years to more than two thousand people.[2] When placed in the context of British church life, this growth is phenomenal. Church attendance in Britain has been declining since 1916. (Thankfully, Protestant church attendance started to grow again in 1989.)

From the beginning, they wove together evangelism and social ministry. Roger had seen many churches run by pastors and teachers with no evangelistic zeal, so one principle of the new church was that, in Roger's words, "anybody in senior leadership in the church had to have either an evangelistic ministry or an evangelistic heart."

For most of the first few years, Faith ran their ministry to the needy. Jesus Action, as they still call it, was not large, complex, or political. They simply offered practical, concrete help to anybody who saw their Jesus-Action number posted all around the neighborhood and called for assistance. They helped with gardening, shopping, baby-sitting, or visiting the elderly, the disabled, or single parents. People without transportation could get a free ride to the hospital.

They never forced Jesus on those they served. In fact, Faith says, "We don't go in and start pushing them to become Christians." But eventually, people often asked questions. And many have come to faith in Christ.

One day a woman who had just left a psychiatric hospital called the Jesus Action number. A single parent, she needed to shop for food and wash her clothes, and she didn't know how to get her six-year-old into school. Somewhere she had seen the Jesus-Action number that Ichthus posts everywhere. "Is this Jesus

Action?" she asked Faith over the telephone. "Yes," Faith responded. "Well," the woman went on, "I want the action, but I don't want the Jesus. I don't want anyone coming around here ramming religion down my throat." Faith assured her that would not happen. After Faith helped her with the washing and shopping, the woman invited her to sit down for a cup of tea. A mere ten minutes later, the woman blurted out: "Okay, what's all this about Jesus?" Teasingly, Faith reminded her, "We had an arrangement before I came that I'm not going to shove religion down your throat." But the woman insisted. So Faith shared the Gospel and prayed with her.

Often—although not always—that kind of evangelistic opportunity resulted from their simple caring for people's needs. Every three months, they had a supper for all who had been helped in Jesus Action. Afterward, they shared the Gospel. Some began to come to church as a result. The church began to grow steadily.

Fellowship, training, and mission have been the three central concerns of this expanding church.

Fellowship

Roger's longing for a New Testament church with genuine caring and community has shaped Ichthus's common life. Ichthus emphasizes corporate leadership, and intimate, open caring among that leadership. Roger believes Jesus gave us a clear promise in John 17:20–23: non-Christians will be able to recognize believers as Jesus' disciples because they love each other. Roger's conclusion is simple: "If we cannot do that in the leadership, then we have no right to teach anybody else." Major decisions are made corporately by a central leadership team where Roger is "first among equals."

Of course, no church is perfect, and Icthus does not pretend to be, either. The leaders have had their fair share of problems (including disciplinary issues with people in positions of responsibility). But they still hold to the ideals of openness and mutual accountability.

Ichthus is organized to maximize intimate fellowship.

Everyone in Ichthus belongs to a house group (twenty-plus people) or neighborhood group, as they are now called. Neighborhood group leaders have a strong pastoral responsibility to nurture and disciple the members of their group.[3]

Several neighborhood groups make up each of the thirty congregations now scattered across Greater London. These congregations, each led by a leadership team, meet on Sunday morning three times a month. On the other Sunday, the neighborhood groups meet separately for fellowship. Then, two Sunday evenings a month, the entire Ichthus Fellowship assembles for what they call "Celebrations." They sing (often with the music of Graham Kendrick) and worship together, praising God in the gently charismatic atmosphere that characterizes all of Ichthus's life and ministry. Every quarter, there is a celebration on Saturday evening so they can invite other churches to join them.

Ichthus has never considered it right to invest much money in buildings. (Their ever-expanding mission has too many financial needs.) They have a modest office building and a prayer center where they seek to have round-the-clock intercession for their many ministries as well as the needs of others. But they have always rented facilities for worship—large halls in schools, unused church buildings, whatever was available. The oldest congregation, Forest Hill, which Roger and Faith lead, worships in the Bonhoeffer Memorial Church, renting space for Sunday worship from a small Lutheran congregation that Dietrich Bonhoeffer pastored before he returned to Germany to help challenge Hitler. Another congregation uses a Baptist church and is officially a member of both Ichthus and the Baptist Union. (Denominational structures never prevent Ichthus from doing what it feels called to do!)

At the center of Ichthus Fellowship, structurally, is a leadership team of nine leaders, including Faith and Roger. All of these nine are actively engaged in a leadership team in one of the thirty congregations, which are organized geographically. There are also thirteen departments of Ichthus that relate to the whole fellowship. These include departments on training, pastoral care, prayer, children, youth, and so forth. Each of the nine central leaders is responsible for one or two of these departments.

Perhaps the most surprising fact about this central leadership team is that two of the people are women. Women, in fact, occupy leadership roles at every level of the fellowship. Women lead one-fifth to one-quarter of the churches, and many women lead neighborhood groups. Ichthus believes in the full participation of women in the church.

Faith Forster's own journey here is fascinating. She is certainly not a militant feminist, but long ago she rejected stereotyping based on gender. In primary school, she raised a fuss when the teachers automatically assumed that all the little girls would take sewing classes and all the little boys would study woodworking. After she won the right to choose, she chose sewing! At age seventeen, she won two young men to Christ and discipled them. Then after they went to Bible school, they informed her that she had no right to do such things.

By the time she and Roger married, Faith had a strong sense of call to Christian ministry. Fortunately, Roger supported her call. In the earliest years of Ichthus, Faith did everything Roger did. During his frequent travels, the other leaders often looked to her for direction, but when they selected elders, they were all men.

The problem finally crystalized about 1979. Ichthus was trying to improve its internal management, so they put the leadership structure on paper. Every active person had a box except Faith! When she asked the person who had drawn up the detailed chart where she belonged, he was startled. He insisted she belonged up at the top beside Roger. Faith objected, "I don't lead this church. But I do quite a lot. So please put me in a box somewhere. Let me belong somewhere."

Finally, after several years' studying and an interim arrangement where Faith became a deacon, Ichthus decided to recognize women as well as men as elders. Full participation of women at every level of church life is now a regular part of Ichthus's teaching and practice. For a time, Faith led a whole area of Ichthus with nine congregations and eleven full-time workers. Faith has also been a member of the executive committee of the British Evangelical Alliance for a number of years. The fact that she has been the only woman in that body underlines how unusual Ichthus Fellowship still is in the evangelical community.

In many different ways, Ichthus Fellowship reflects Roger's

love for the sixteenth-century Anabaptists. Ichthus's theology is Arminian rather than Calvinist. They teach non-violence. Community is central to their understanding of the church. A concern for simplicity pervades their personal and church lifestyle at every level. Roger is one of the very few persons who has walked in procession in Westminster Abbey wearing ordinary street clothes while all the other church dignitaries around him were adorned in proper ecclesiastical robes. Why? "I believe in an inspirational church, not institutions," Roger replies. "Institutions wear robes. Inspirational people just wear their work clothes."

Training

Training is central to the life of Ichthus. Startrite is their initial discipling program for new Christians. Since many of their members are new converts with little or no understanding of Christianity, they had to develop a basic discipling program. Startrite has shaped the faith of hundreds of new Christians, and has been translated into a number of different languages.

Ichthus also runs a training program for more mature Christians (minimum age: twenty-three). Network is a year-long program that combines biblical and theological work with practical involvement in the life of Ichthus. Trainees are involved in one of Ichthus's local neighborhood groups and participate in their evangelism and social ministry. Since Network started in 1982, nearly two hundred people have gone through the program.[4]

Mission

How has Ichthus grown from fourteen members to more than two thousand in fewer than twenty years? Because they believe passionately in evangelism. They do it constantly—in almost every imaginable way.

When you ask Roger about Ichthus's evangelistic methods, he responds: "We use everything. Stand on your head in the middle of the street if necessary to get attention." They sometimes go door-to-door. They hold open-air evangelistic meetings in the streets. They invite people to parties to buy Third World crafts

(Roger is a vice-president of Tear Fund, a large evangelical relief and development agency.) They perform pantomimes in local theaters. They witness through all the variety of social ministries that have developed. After one of their regular meals for the elderly, an old woman said "Oh, if God's like that, I want more of him."

The good work of Jesus Action continues to open doors and hearts. One week, Jesus Action volunteers helped clean up for a ninety-year-old woman whose apartment had been flooded. A couple days later, her granddaughter Valerie, came looking for them. "Are you the people who dried out Grandma?" Valerie asked. When they said they were, Valerie said simply, "I want to become a Christian."

Ian King, a leader of the Downham congregation, talked about the many things they did to become friends with their neighbors—anything "to bring people from outside into contact with people in the church and just let conversations develop." Sunday services in the park, video parties in homes, and a Christmas float have all worked. For Christmas 1992 they organized a live band to travel around the neighborhood on a large truck, playing secular as well as Christian Christmas songs. They gave out Christmas cards to everyone and candy to the children and invited people to their Christmas service.

Every third Saturday, Ian and others from the congregation do an open-air event in the streets. They play instruments, sing, preach a bit, and hand out flyers about the church. Recently, a young woman who lived above the stores where they were conducting the open-air meeting listened for a time, then came down into the street and asked how to become a Christian. She has been attending church regularly. Three older women liked the freedom and joy of the open-air celebrations so much that they, too, have started coming to the church. They are also encouraging their friends to come as well. One has become a Christian.

It would be impossible to say whether Ichthus's "Brown Bear Pub" falls under the category of evangelism or social action. It started because the fellowship wanted to minister to youth in London's Deptford district—an area full of drugs, violence, homelessness, and racial tension.

All along they had hoped to develop a church that was culturally relevant for young people. The pub seemed to be the right place. A thriving youth church has developed in the first two years of the ministry at the pub. They are creating music that is neither white nor black. A dozen or so converts from the community have joined with Ichthus youth from other congregations to form Ichthus's only youth church of about seventy kids. Eventually they hope to buy equipment and open a fitness center for young people, but for the present, the pub is open every day of the week and on Friday evening—as a church.

Their weekly service is on Friday evening. They dance, sing, discuss issues such as sex and drugs, and pray for each other. Teenagers often preach. Teenagers lead the six house groups that meet each week. Some Ichthus youth on the periphery of other congregations have found a place to be active leaders. David Westlake, the leader, helps kids get off drugs or find a place to live. About a dozen teenagers from the area accepted Christ in the first two years.

While John[5] was walking past one day, the Brown Bear's sign stating "non-alcoholic pub" caught his attention. John had lived a hard life. His mother was often drunk, and his dad regularly beat him up. John found consolation in drugs. At age twelve, he assaulted a police officer. He was thrown out of school when he climbed up on the school roof, threw slate tiles at the teachers, and then came down and beat up a teacher. Stealing cars was John's way to make money.

Soon after visiting the Brown Bear, John went to an Ichthus youth retreat. When he started to pray, he fell on the ground as other teenagers prayed for him in tongues. Someone asked him if he wanted to become a Christian. "Yeah, all right, I'll give it a go," John responded. Today he adds, "And I ain't got in trouble since." John continues to struggle, but his life is dramatically changed.

Gaza[6] also came to Christ at the Brown Bear. Her mother is Jamaican and her dad is Nigerian, but they are divorced. Fighting and stealing were a regular part of Gaza's life. Fortunately, one of Gaza's classmates at school was a member of Ichthus and invited her to come to church at the Brown Bear. Slowly, over a number of months, she came to accept Christ. Martin Young, one of the adult leaders at the Brown Bear says that Gaza "gradually became a Christian." Gaza still has tough problems to deal with at home. Her mother frequently brings in drunk boyfriends. Her brothers bring in girlfriends with their babies. Gaza still gets into trouble at school sometimes, but God is slowly taking away the rage inside. "What is lovely," Martin says, "is that you see Jesus gradually changing her in a very gentle way. And now she gets up and preaches and prays and has prophecies for people."

Some black youth attend the Brown Bear church, but not in as large a proportion as in the surrounding neighborhood. The same is true of Ichthus generally. They have significant numbers of nonwhites in some of their churches. An African, Kofi Osafo, is a member of the central leadership team. His wife, Yvonne, leads one of the congregations. Ichthus has worked hard to be racially inclusive. The fellowship is a member not only of the (largely white) Evangelical Alliance but also of the (largely black) Afro-Caribbean Evangelical Alliance. But Ichthus generally and the Brown Bear Youth Church in particular are actively seeking to become more thoroughly multi-racial.

The Kettle of Fish Theatre Group is another reminder that Ichthus uses many different evangelistic methods. Mark and Karen Cavallini, who now lead the group, both studied drama in university. Dismayed with the kind of superficial drama most Christians do, they resolved to do better. Begun in 1991, Kettle of Fish already has experienced substantial success. Twice they have been part of the Greenwich Festival, the largest secular-arts festival in London.

They first got started with street theatre in Soho, London's central red-light district. One day a man from Scotland wandered in and accepted Christ after watching their pantomime in a hall between two houses of prostitution.

Later, Mark and Karen helped plant a church among the working-class folk of the housing estates in Islington. They used short drama sketches and rock-and-roll songs. They are ardent fans of Tony Campolo and love his line that "the Kingdom of God is a party." So they found a large truck, assembled balloons, streamers, clowns, and bears, and toured the neighborhood with music. There were fifteen converts in a six-month period. So they started a new congregation.

Today Kettle of Fish performs most often in "Jack's Basement." (Jack's Basement is another Ichthus ministry that offers three Friday evenings a month, a wide variety of artistic events including drama, music, painting, architecture, and dance—in a low-key way so the unchurched feel comfortable). That seems to be an ideal setting for reaching the trendy, theater-going Greenwich crowd. They also perform in pubs, community centers, outdoors, and in government schools. Often the audiences are not Christian. They write many of their own plays, developing drama that contains a biblical message without being "preachy" or explicitly Christian. "We feel we can bring a Christian worldview or viewpoint into peoples' lives," Karen says, "and also just bring the Holy Spirit into a place without necessarily performing material that is specifically Christian."

Michael[7] is the brother of one of Mark and Karen's close friends in Ichthus. Michael was intensely anti-Christian but desperately wanted to get into sound and lighting in the Theatre, so he accepted Mark and Karen's offer to do that for one of the stagings of their popular play, *Mary Magdalene*. He watched as they prayed and worshiped at length (as they always do) before each rehearsal and performance. On the last night of the play, Michael accepted Christ.

Like Kettle of Fish and many other Ichthus programs, the "Over-Sixties' Club" and the "Mothers and Toddlers Group" also weave together low-key friendship evangelism and social ministry in a subtle, effective way. They are conscious attempts to bring Christians into supportive, relaxed contact with non-Christians. In fact, that may be one of the most important parts of Ichthus's evangelistic strategy.

When they started the Downham congregation, they realized that little was happening for the many elderly residents of the old council estates nearby. In the words of one of Downham congregation's leaders, Ian King, they wanted "a nice place [where] people could go to have a coffee and have a chat and just enjoy." So they operate the "Over-Sixties' Club" every Wednesday morning. Every other week a speaker from one of the Ichthus congregations comes in to talk about a topic of interest to seniors—a policeman on security or someone knowledgeable about depression or hospice care. They come in as specialists, but they always weave in their faith in Jesus. Over a few years, about eight people have become Christians through the "Over-Sixties' Club."

The "Mothers and Toddlers Group" is similar. It offers a friendly setting for neighborhood women to come in on Thursday morning and have coffee. Their children have fun with the toys Ichthus supplies, while they chat with Christian mothers from the Downham congregation.

One leader who started a new congregation took a job for a time as a local milkman. Sometimes they joke that he was probably "the highest-educated milkman in England." But he sure got to know local people!

In a whole variety of ways, Ichthus consciously seeks for ways for Ichthus members to meet non-Christian neighbors in a friendly, relaxed, "non-churchy" context. That is true of the Brown Bear Pub, the Kettle of Fish Theatre group, the Over-Sixties' Club, and many other programs.

Ichthus' zeal for evangelism extends to the whole world. By 1993, they had seventy-four people serving outside Great Britain in evangelistic work. The Middle East is their area of special focus. Ichthus related missionaries also serve in France, Germany, Albania, Hong Kong, Pakistan, South America, and Central Asia.

Ichthus' theology does not distinguish between evangelism and social action. The mission of the church is evangelism and that must be done using words, works, and wonders.[8] Not every act of social concern, of course, is evangelism. It must be done by Christians in the power of the Holy Spirit. When that happens, they understand it as an incarnation of Jesus in their neighborhoods. Such works reveal God as a caring Father (Matt. 5:16), but without the Holy Spirit good works merely draw attention to the human agent. "Anything that we might loosely call social action," Roger says, "is really in our theory evangelism. Everything that we are doing is releasing the Holy Spirit into society—whether it's with our words, whether it's with our works and deeds, or whether it's with signs and wonders."

Ichthus is clearly charismatic. The gifts of healing, tongues, and prophecy are all present in the fellowship. Roger, Faith, and Graham Kendrick are internationally recognized charismatic leaders. But Roger is aware of the weaknesses of the movement: "It is not too difficult to identify and even to despise some charismatics' self-indulgence and self-interest. While they are praying, no doubt legitimately, for the removal of their latest bunion or cold, thousands of their fellow humans pass into eternity through lack of nourishment. Thousands more are being exploited by political and economic oppression." Ichthus is a charismatic fellowship that uses the gifts of the Holy Spirit for wholistic evangelism that weaves together preaching, social ministry, and miraculous signs to lead people to Christ.

Today, Ichthus operates a large number of social ministries in crisis pregnancy, job training, schools, Third World crafts, and political engagement. But they are all tied to the fellowship's evangelistic concerns. In fact, they virtually all started as projects of individual congregations that responded to immediate need. As Ann Handford says, "We can't be the people of God and say 'Jesus loves you,' for example, in Soho, without doing something about homelessness and the prostitutes."

Until recently, Ann was the Executive Director of Ichthus Community Projects (ICP). She used to work for Shell Oil. A few years ago, she decided she really didn't care very much if people buy gasoline from Shell or British Petroleum, so she took the job of heading up ICP—a separate legal entity that oversees the legal and financial concerns for Ichthus's community projects. Spiritual accountability for the projects, however, remains with the local congregations. The reason is simple: Ichthus is very concerned to make sure that their social action never gets divorced from the life of the church.

Hilltop Crisis Pregnancy Center offers support to women (and also, occasionally, to the fathers!) who have unwanted pregnancies. They also teach sex-education classes in government schools. Jenny Thomas, the director, is a full-time paid staff person, but most of the other twenty staff are volunteers from the Crystal Palace congregation that started the program and takes basic responsibility for it. A team of intercessors pray regularly for the work. Each counselor has a special intercessor who is called when the counselor faces a special problem.

Mike Pears's congregation in Peckham and Camberwell runs

two nursery schools and a primary school to serve their inner-city neighborhood. The people living in the many surrounding government-owned apartment buildings suffer constant vandalism, crime, and high unemployment. (In one of the housing estates where they work, the unemployment rate is thirty-eight percent!) Over fifty percent of the children live in single-parent families. The schools in the area do not rate well in the current government report.

The two nursery schools (twenty-five kids each) and a beginning elementary school were begun to meet these desperate needs. Staff wages are very low so that even the poorest parents can afford to send their children.

Fees vary according to the parents' income. The elementary school started by popular demand a couple of years after the nursery schools began. The people were so pleased with the nursery schools that they begged the church to start an elementary school so their children could continue with the same quality of teaching and concern.

Ichthus had a second reason for starting the primary school. Ichthus's Christian families with young children were feeling great pressure to move out of the inner city because they wanted quality education for their children. Ichthus's goal, Mike Pears says, is "to retake the inner cities." So they started the elementary school both for their non-Christian neighbors and for themselves.

Regular evenings of intercessory prayer by the staff are an important part of the work of the schools. One evening the staff of one of the nursery schools prayed especially for one of the little girls in the nursery. They knew that the little girl's mother was neglecting the child because of her live-in boyfriend. The child was doing badly at school, but the staff said nothing to the mother. They simply prayed. The next week the mother showed up unannounced and said, "I have thrown my boyfriend out. I have decided from now on that I'm going to put my daughter first in my life." In fact, she went on to tell them that she had noticed that her little daughter was far happier at nursery school than at home. "Could you teach me to make her happy at home like she is at nursery?" she pleaded.

That is how they do low-key friendship evangelism through

the schools. That mother has attended church a couple of times, although she is not yet a Christian. A couple of other parents have come to Christ. Large events for parents every term enable them to meet staff and other church members. The staff are not yet satisfied with the evangelistic impact of the schools. They plan to introduce a class for parents of children in the elementary school to explain the goals and philosophy of the school.

Mike Pears believes they are engaged in low-profile spiritual warfare. "Not only in the sense of standing in a room and shouting at the principalities and power," he said. "But in the sense that when the staff in Ichthus's schools pray, stand for family life, and teach the children about Jesus Christ in a context where the powers of evil have become very powerful, they are waging spiritual warfare. The influence of a nursery school can be much greater than just the sum of contacts with individual families."

The Peckham Evangelical Churches' Action Network (PECAN) is a $375,000-a-year program to help the long-term unemployed get back to work. An independent board composed of Christians from a number of churches controls PECAN. But the fellowship started PECAN and two thirds of the staff are members of Ichthus.

In Peckham, with its many huge government-owned apartments, the official unemployment rate is thirty-eight percent. Government unemployment programs don't have a very good record. In terms of money spent and people who find jobs, PECAN is five times more successful.

PECAN's seventeen staff members offer twenty courses each year to help the unemployed get ready for a job. Each course lasts four weeks. In 1991, three hundred-sixty unemployed persons participated. Sixty percent of them found jobs or went on to further job training.

PECAN works because it is more flexible and more personal than similar government programs. Graduates often comment on the striking contrast between how PECAN and government programs treat people. PECAN's director, Simon Pellew, believes that is a reflection of the Christian commitments that undergird PECAN.

PECAN is open to everyone. Christian faith is not an explicit part of the program. But somewhere in every course, the staff speak about their faith and indicate that PECAN is a Christian organization. All staff are committed Christians. They pray together every day over lunch. Once every five weeks, the staff spend a whole afternoon praying together. PECAN also sponsors a quarterly meeting of prayer to encourage churches to pray for their work.

PECAN does not engage in direct evangelism. But Simon understands PECAN as low-key spiritual warfare challenging "the principalities and powers that dominate Peckham. I see that as demonic power as well as an oppressive local government, . . . unemployment, family break-up, and child abuse."

Simon's relationship with Maureen[9] reflects PECAN's approach. Maureen was full of anger at parents who had placed her in a convent and never visited. She had little self-esteem. Day after day, Simon observed her inner pain and her anguish, and he began to pray regularly for an opportunity to talk with her.

One day, Simon prayed specifically that he would have a chance that day to talk with Maureen during a class trip to a business. Maureen was always early for class. But that day she arrived late, uptight, and ready to explode. The others had already left. When Simon asked if she wanted to talk, she burst into tears. She knew God only as an impersonal force and a harsh disciplinarian. She wanted love. After Simon explained God's love for her, she was glad to have him pray for her. She talked frequently to Simon over the next weeks and joined an Ichthus class for inquirers. She now attends service regularly and believes that apart from her new faith in Christ she would not be alive today.

Ichthus not only meets immediate human need. The leadership also understands the importance of politics. Petitions to government officials, lobbying, personal friendships with politicians, and intercessory prayer on specific political issues—all have been used in their political work.

One of their more dramatic battles happened when a local government in an Ichthus borough introduced curricula in the schools (even the nursery and primary schools) promoting a gay lifestyle. They leafletted the entire borough, and Roger Forster read Romans 1 to a committee of the local council of the borough.

There was sound and fury for a time. Local newspapers denounced them as dangerous cultists. They lost government money for a proposed job-training program. Eventually they took their concerns to the national government, which later passed legislation prohibiting local-government money from being used to promote a homosexual lifestyle.

Ichthus's political engagement, however, does not end with issues like homosexuality and abortion. They have also petitioned the government to support increased funds for poor nations and to be more concerned for human rights. They have lobbied the British government to keep its promise to increase foreign economic aid to 0.7 percent of GNP, pointing out that their fellowship does far more than that. They oppose Sunday trading, but not on narrow religious grounds. "We simply stand with the trade unions on the issue," Roger says. They agree with the unions that Sunday trading will harm workers.

Ichthus's political engagement is not a sustained, highly organized activity. As in all other areas of their life and mission, they try to listen to the Spirit and move when they feel led. The result is certainly not a narrow "right-wing" agenda. Roger insists that "Jesus seems committed equally to condemning fornication and divorce as to warning rich oppressors." (Matt. 19:9, Luke 6:24–25). "It is difficult to see the abortion issue in any light other than that of the bomb, where wholesale slaughter of the innocents is also at stake." That kind of balanced agenda has been attacked not only by left-wingers in the local council but also by conservative Christians. Roger acknowledges that those who are committed to "giving women equal place, helping the poor, and repudiating violence in the world are identified with liberalism, feminism, pacifism, and communism."[10] Even the New Age Movement! But they persist in trying to follow a biblically informed political agenda, no matter whom it offends.

Ichthus has a variety of other social ministries. Just Trading sells Third World handicrafts and offers justice education about global trade and poverty. Houses into Homes (which is just beginning) hopes to use some of the many vacant homes to provide a context for offering inexpensive housing and mentoring disturbed people. A recently organized credit union both encourages the poor to save and offers them loans at lower interest rates.

Not all Ichthus programs succeed. Since they depend on volunteers, they start, thrive, or fail, depending on the interest and skill of those volunteers. Sometimes outside factors also cause failure. The first attempt to start what eventually became PECAN collapsed because of intense hostility from the local government council furious over Ichthus's stand on homosexuality. More recently a thriving launderette failed because of crime and vandalism.

Pecan opened the launderette in 1990 on a large Peckham Council estate full of crime, cockroaches, drugs, graffitti, and litter. Before they opened, residents had to walk half a mile to the nearest launderette. After a $75,000 renovation job, the launderette quickly became an important meeting place for the community. It provided a clean place where residents could chat over coffee, and children could buy candy.

It was also a place to meet needy persons like Paul.[11] Paul was a violent, angry resident who regularly used the launderette. Each evening he sat obsessed in his apartment, cleaning and sharpening a whole row of knives. Paul had designated each knife to kill a specific person. One day he shouted, "God—if there is a God—you've got to tell me today because if you don't tell me today, I'm killing myself." Desperate, he walked into the launderette. The person in charge talked with him and then took him to Simon. That day, Paul accepted Christ. He has stopped drugs, drinking, and beating his wife, and has been baptized.

In spite of its initial success, trouble also started early. Violent youths burglarized the launderette several times. When Simon and the manager of the launderette confronted employees stealing one hundred-fifty dollars a month, they almost got killed. The girl's father attacked them with a knife, chased them to their car, and smashed their windows as they tried to leave. Mysteriously, after jumping into the back seat and shouting to the manager, "You're a dead man," he suddenly walked away. No one was hurt, but Simon decided he had to close down the launderette. In war zones like the Peckham Council estates, even good ministries sometimes fail.

Ichthus Fellowship has become a gift, not only to southeast

London but also to the world. People come from many countries to study in their training programs. Their musician, Graham Kendrick, writes some of the best contemporary Christian music. Their missionaries are in many nations. And the Marches for Jesus, which started in Ichthus, are now an annual event in scores of nations around the world.[12]

The Marches for Jesus had their origins in the prayer walks[13] that Ichthus regularly used to begin their congregations. When they started the church in Soho, London's major prostitution center, in 1985, three hundred Christians paraded around Soho, singing praises to God and praying that God would defeat the powers of evil. To their amazement, many prostitutes poured out of the houses, cheering and urging them to sing for them. That march soon led to a larger one around London's central business district. Soon, hundreds of thousands of Christians were marching first across England, then Europe, then the United States. The year 1994 saw the first global March for Jesus, with millions of Christians marching in more than one hundred-seventy nations.

The marches provide an opportunity for large numbers of Christians from diverse denominational backgrounds to witness publicly to the Lordship of Christ and pray together for the defeat of the powers of evil. Roger Forster and Graham Kendrick continue to play a major role in the Marches for Jesus, but Ichthus Fellowship in no way tries to control them. They are now a global phenomenon that God chose to begin in a very special fellowship in a poorer section of London.

Ichthus Fellowship is an amazing body that defies all normal categories. It sees itself as evangelical, charismatic, Anabaptist, and above all, biblical. It combines evangelism and social concern, immersing them both in prayer, fasting, and a fervent, expectant dependence on the awesome presence of the Holy Spirit. And it continues to grow—in numbers, biblical depth, and global impact.

---

1   Eventually, the Marches for Jesus became national·and then international. Gerald Coates and Lynn Green are codirectors along with Roger Forster and Graham Kendrick.

2   The congregation developed in Forest Hill, a twilight zone between depressed inner-city areas like Peckham and more affluent districts like Bromley.

3 See Roger Forster's chapter, "Ichthus Christian Fellowship," in *Ten New Churches*, ed. Roger Forster (MARC Europe, 1986), 60–63.

4 A shorter summer program for two to four weeks enables younger Christians to profit from the same combination during the summer.

5 I have changed his name.

6 I have changed her name.

7 I have changed his name.

8 See Roger Forster's article on Ichthus Fellowship in *Transformation*, April-June 1992, 15.

9 I have changed her name.

10 "Roger's Write," *Celebrations*, September 1991, 4. See also Roger's comments in *Transformation*, April/June, 1992, 16.

11 I have changed his name.

12 For a short popular history, see Graham Kendrick, Gerald Coates, Roger Forster, and Lynn Green, *March for Jesus* (Eastbourne: Kingsway Publications, 1992).

13 See Graham Kendrick and John Houghton, *Prayerwalking* (Eastbourne: Kingsway Publications, 1990).

3
From the Halls of Cambridge to the Slums of Bangalore

We must see Christ in the disturbing disguise of the poor.

Mother Teresa

Vinay and Colleen Samuel were comfortable, British-educated, middle-class Indian Christians. They served the most prestigious Episcopal church in one of India's large cities. Why would they choose to move their whole family to the slums? How did that nurture a ministry that built several churches and now serves fifty thousand poor people? And why did the people of Bangalore (a city of over four million in southern India) ask Colleen to run for mayor and the Indian parliament?

Colleen and Vinay are two of the most unusual people I know.

The daughter of a well-to-do businessman, Colleen attended elite schools and then married Vinay, the brilliant young minister who joined the pastoral team at prestigious St. John's Episcopal church, Bangalore in 1967. Vinay also grew up in a middle-class family where servants cared for his needs. With excellent Western-style education, they both fit easily into British university life while Vinay did graduate study at Cambridge University from 1972–75.

In 1975, God called Vinay and Colleen back to St. John's Bangalore. Now senior pastor of this large, middle-class Indian congregation, Vinay was very busy. Senior officers of the Indian army, navy, and airforce attended his church. But protocol demanded that when their thirty-three-year-old pastor entered the room, these top military leaders would stand. Secretly, Vinay confesses, he rather enjoyed it! By 1978, however, Colleen says, "We felt absolutely frustrated and depressed with our lifestyle of being involved only with those who were financially stable."[1]

For many years, God had been preparing Colleen and Vinay to work with the poor. As a child, Colleen enjoyed comfort and security as the daughter of a successful businessman. But even then, she remembers, she used to wake up in the night during torrential monsoon rains and worry about the poor living in rain-drenched huts. When she surrendered her life to Christ in her late teens, God immediately gave her a strong desire to serve the "unlovely, silent, marginalized and under-privileged."

Vinay was moving in the same direction. He studied India's poverty from 1969–1972 when he taught at Union Biblical Seminary in central India. The fiery words of the prophets always made him uncomfortable about the state of the poor. However, he was also very uncomfortable with the emerging "ecumenical" options for social action which appeared to distort the Gospel he longed to share with all who did not know Christ.

In 1975, Colleen began to spend two hours a day in Lingarajapuram, a slum on the outskirts of Bangalore. With some support from affluent St. John's, she started a school for very poor children unable to afford an education. Desperate need was everywhere. Soon Colleen and Vinay and the community development association they organized were operating not only a school, but orphanages, job training programs and health clinics. They also planted a church in Lingarajapuram which by 1987 had grown to about two hundred families.

In 1983, Vinay and Colleen surprised both the middle-class Christians at St. John's and the slum dwellers in Lingarajapuram. Their whole family moved to the slum. Vinay exchanged the pastorate of prestigious St. John's for the new, rapidly growing church in Lingarajapuram. Why this move? "The only motivation," Colleen responds, "has been and will always be the person of Jesus Christ."

Lingarajapuram is a teeming unzoned area just to the north of India's fastest growing city, Bangalore. At any time of day, long lines of ox-carts, trucks, scooters, buses, cars, and pedestrians jostle for space at the narrow railway crossing on the rail line that divides Lingarajapuram from the city. Since it is outside city limits, it has no piped water or official street cleaning. Small stores and workshops open to the street and line the main road. One-

and two-story brick houses spring up almost randomly as people build without permits on unlicensed land.

Behind the brick houses stretch vast numbers of humbler dwellings—many one-room sheds (10 by 15 feet in size) made of mud and leaves with doorways so small one must crawl through the "door." Once inside, there is room only to squat. These tiny huts are home not only to fifty percent of Lingarajapuram's eighty-five thousand people, but also to most of the members of an extraordinary church, Divya Shanthi—the House of Peace.

Of Lingarajapuram's eighty-five thousand people, fifty percent are poor and twenty percent are desperately poor. Thirty percent of the children receive little or no education. Sanitation is primitive. One understaffed state school caters to five hundred children. A government medical clinic is run by a nurse when she happens to attend.

After they moved here, Colleen and Vinay plunged even more deeply into the work of their growing wholistic community development association called the Divya Shanthi Christian Association (DSCA). "Divya Shanthi" means "peace of God." The name, Vinay explains, points to that "wholeness, shalom, and community reconciliation that God intends for all communities." Vinay has been the President of DSCA and Colleen the Executive Director. Today DSCA has two hundred-fifty paid staff who provide a vast array of programs to a largely Hindu and Muslim population of about fifty thousand persons.

By the summer of 1992, programs and staff were working so well that the Samuels were able to move to Oxford for a much-deserved sabbatical. They did not slow down much, of course. Colleen is working on a Ph.D., and Vinay finally has time for more writing.

At Lingarajapuram, Colleen was the "on-site" manager, in part because Vinay was often gone on international travel. In fact, Vinay quips, "Colleen practices what I preach." Vinay is not only a local pastor and community-development organizer. He is also an internationally prominent Christian leader and theologian. He has been active in the World Evangelical Fellowship, the Lausanne Committee for World Evangelization and the World Council of Churches, bridging the gap between ecumenical social activists and evangelical church planters. A theologian who stresses the dignity of the poor, Vinay has organized international conferences and organizations focused on combining evangelism and social justice.

So sometimes, Vinay was abroad when things got tough. But Colleen is, in the words of one of her colleagues, an "iron lady" who has "more courage than a man." She has walked into the middle of a group of fighting men and separated them. She took on the local prostitution rings and defied their threat to kidnap her children.

Prayer is her anchor—not just thirty minutes at the beginning of the day, but regular prayer—as Colleen says, "individual prayer sent up in whispers as one goes about on the streets or in homes or government offices." Colleen believes her strength comes from her constant communication with God—"almost a minute by minute reliance on Him whether consciously or unconsciously all through the day." Especially in times of tension, she has discovered that "to acknowledge that the work is God's and that you are not on your own makes all the difference."

The people love Colleen. They have begged her to run for mayor of Bangalore, for the state parliament, and even for the national parliament of India. She always declined, although she probably would have won. Her calling was elsewhere. And when one looks at the range of ministries she and Vinay have organized through the Divya Shanthi Christian Association, one understands.

DSCA's programs fall into five areas: schools; child care; community development; economic development; and spiritual life, worship, and evangelism.

DSCA's schools started under a tree in 1967. When Colleen visited the slums of Lingarajapuram, she met poor kids roaming the streets because they could not afford the fees or clothes for school. So Colleen gathered some children under a tree and started to teach them.

Today Miss Chandra Ponnurangam oversees the education department where one thousand students study in nursery, primary, and secondary schools. There is also a "special needs" class for thirty-five mentally handicapped kids.

One day the police brought a badly battered, mentally disabled little eight-year-old boy to DSCA. He seemed to be abandoned and penniless. Unable to find a home for him, they started a special class for him and other kids like him from very poor homes. They named him *Kumar*, which means "prince." Six months later a bank manager walked in looking for his son who had wandered away from a prestigious school for the mentally handicapped. The father was overjoyed that his son was receiving such loving care.

DSCA's schools transform lives. At fifteen, Norbert's future looked hopeless. He had no education. His dad was unemployed. Three siblings were mentally handicapped. Then, at fifteen, Norbert entered one of DSCA's schools. He learned to read and write and then proceeded to the engineering center. Along with everyone else in DSCA's schools, he also took part in daily prayers and studied the Bible. Today, Norbert has a living faith in Jesus Christ. His new self-respect and confidence have also spread to other members of the family. His sister Sharon found a job and now proudly cares for her father and mother. The grandmother brings the three mentally handicapped children to DSCA's "special needs" school—one of them has begun to speak. Is it any wonder that Norbert's mother is known for her joyful singing of hymns?

One day in 1981, Colleen saw Muniappa and two other little boys scavenging in garbage cans for food. When they begged for money, she offered something better: "Don't ask for money. Be ready tomorrow morning, and I'll bring you to school." So at age ten, Muniappa started to study at DSCA's school. Today he is a small-businessman building homes.

A variety of child-care programs led by Gerry Bastian, are a second major area of DSCA's ministry. Three hundred children live in four boarding homes. Twenty-two babies received care in their Baby Saving Shelter from 1987–1992. The Family Helper Program assists four hundred-fifty children living at home in very poor families. Clothes, books, health care, and special classes for their parents in family planning, values, and economic improvement, work together to change lives.

The boarding home for girls started when a girl came to Colleen begging for help to avoid prostitution. (Many desperately poor families in India sell their daughters as prostitutes.) This young girl wept as she explained that her older sister was already a prostitute and her mother planned to force her to do the same. "I don't want to go home tonight, you've got to take me into a hostel," she told Colleen. But DSCA didn't have any boarding house! Instead, Colleen took her to her own home that night.

The very next day, entirely out of the blue, Colleen received a telephone call to say that a visitor from Holland wanted to visit their school. When she arrived, Colleen learned that Mrs. Rookmaaker represented the Save the Children Fund that sponsored destitute children in boarding homes. Colleen thanked God and proceeded to develop the boarding homes that offer loving residential care for extremely needy girls and boys.

Rajah is one of these fortunate ones. His parents were stonebreakers—poor manual laborers who do back-breaking work swinging heavy sledgehammers to crush the rock in a stone quarry. They lost their jobs and home when Rajah's older brother defied social boundaries and fell in love with the owner's daughter. Out on the streets with no income, Rajah's mother in desperation took him and two other children to one of DSCA's boarding homes. Like all the children in the boarding homes, Rajah also attended DSCA's schools. A bright student, he is now in college.

Rajah, however, received more than food, shelter, and a good education at DSCA. He also learned about Christ and became a Christian. So did this entire Hindu family. With joy, Rajah reports that "we all have become Christians and we worship only Jesus Christ."

Devotions, Sunday worship, Bible quizzes, and prayer are central to the life of the boarding homes. These homes, in fact, are one of the major avenues of evangelism at DSCA. They are very careful to respect everyone's religious convictions. (Youth in the boarding homes are baptized only after they receive written parental permission.) But many come to Christ. On Easter Sunday, 1992, Gerry Bastian reports, about a dozen youth from his boarding homes received baptism.

Kumaresh was one of them. His parents were so poor that he was unable to go to school until, at the age of eight, he came to DSCA's boarding home for boys . Ten years later he was ready for college. When he asked his Hindu parents if he could receive baptism at Easter 1992, they agreed.

It is much harder for Kasim who comes from a Muslim family. Kasim is grateful for every aspect of the boarding home where he has lived since he was nine. Had he not come, he would still be illiterate: "I would not know what is India and what is the United States." Kasim also feels drawn to Jesus. When the school or boarding home presents a Christian drama, he always asks to play the role of Christ. He considers himself a Christian, although his father refuses to allow him to be baptized.

Miss Thelma Dawson, retired manager from Hindustan Aeronautics, manages a number of programs in DSCA's Department of Community Development. The adult literacy program teaches seventy to eighty mothers in their homes to read and write. The Doorstep Centers gather together preschoolers (six hundred-thirty in 1992) on doorsteps to prepare them for school. Nurses, doctors, and other health workers in two clinics served over fifty-three-hundred people from July 1991 to June 1992. Clean Green Lingarajapuram is a local cooperative organized by DSCA to collect garbage and sweep the streets. (Because the area is outside Bangalore city limits, the city does not supply these services.)

One of this department's more unusual programs works with the police to help battered women. Frequently a young wife is harassed by her husband's family if she has too small a dowry or fails to bear a son. Beatings, deaths under suspicious circumstances, and suicides are common.

DSCA has developed special programs for these women. A women's group provides support, counsel, and legal advice. When they organized a rally, fifteen hundred women came to discuss the problem with the police. Their cooperative store has a special room set aside to counsel battered women.

DSCA works closely with the police in this program. The police often send women or couples to them for counseling. Eventually, DSCA persuaded the police to set up an entire department in the police force to deal with battered women and dowry harassment. Colleen served on the committee to establish the program and train the police. Colleen also persuaded them to set aside in every police station a special room for counseling women.

Colleen was even appointed as a special police officer. Eventually a bill was introduced into the state legislature, creating a similar program for the police in the whole state.

One day in 1992, the police sent a quarreling Hindu couple to DSCA's women's program. After Colleen helped them work out their disagreements, they returned home together. Two weeks later, they both showed up in church.

Working with oppressed women is important at DSCA. But it would be a mistake to suppose that they neglect the family. In fact, Vinay and Colleen understand the center of their entire program as building the family. "Focus on families has given us a framework of action," Colleen says. "Class struggles, justice fights, liberationist language are all subordinate to the vision of building community as a family and building families in the community."[2]

DSCA also works to establish an economic base among the poor. In 1991, DSCA's production centers exported more than $120,000 worth of goods.

The Women's Work Center provides both training and employment for poor (mostly Hindu) women who might otherwise be forced into prostitution or mistreated in their homes because they lacked economic independence. Each year the center trains twenty-five young women to take the examination for certification in the garment industry. Fees depend on ability to pay, but everyone must contribute something. Since even trainees can produce items for sale, they also receive a modest salary. Some graduates set up their own small business through a special program the center has with the Singer Sewing Machine company. Buying their sewing machine at a thirty-percent discount, the women repay their loans within a year.

The center also employs graduates in its production program, manufacturing school uniforms for DSCA's school children and handmade ties and tea towels for export. Sales in 1992 were $47,000.

As in all of DSCA's programs, work starts with morning devotions. Bible stories and hymn singing frequently add life to the day's sewing routines.

Maheshwari is one of the seamstresses at the Women's Work Center who especially loves the morning devotions and singing.

She first came to DSCA as a child when her mother committed suicide. Colleen took her, along with her brother and sister, into the boarding home. First she studied in DSCA's schools. Then she took the training program in sewing at the Women's Work Center where she now continues to work. She saves some of her income through the center's banking program and cares for her siblings. In July 1992, she was baptized and renamed Elizabeth.

An engineering center provides job training for boys who drop out of school. With its trainees in high demand, it has placed twenty-four young men in engineering jobs in industry since 1984. Another eight have started their own small engineering businesses. Today, the center receives big orders from major companies. John Kaunds, the creative, dedicated engineer who developed this program, bought the center from DSCA in 1993, but he will continue to operate with the same goals of empowering poor boys in the name of Christ.

Developing small businesses through tiny loans is one central way DSCA empowers the poor. In some poor areas, Vinay reports, about seventy percent of the people are self-employed—selling fruit, pulling rickshaws, sewing clothes. They don't want hand-outs, but they cannot afford the money lenders' outrageous interest rates so they are unable to expand their tiny businesses. DSCA's Micro-Business Aide Program offers that capital. They analyze each request to make sure that a loan will be repaid and increase the person's income by twenty-five rupees (about one dollar) a day.

Since 1986, these small loans have improved the lives of two hundred families. By 1992, DSCA was assisting ten tiny businesses per month with micro loans. One of Vinay's greatest joys is providing capital to these very poor entrepreneurs: "To provide capital to them at a reasonable rate of interest and enable them to develop their enterprising qualities and develop as entrepreneurs, and therefore look after themselves, has been one of the most exciting things." The focus of the program is solidarity groups, especially of women who save and are given a matching grant. They use that as capital to assist their members. They make all the decisions and also manage the loans.

DSCA's program in small business development works in

close partnership with David Bussau (see chapter seven). Vinay and David have been close friends since 1978. Together, they help poor people help themselves by offering small loans.

One person who got a loan was a poor Hindu widow who operated a tiny grocery store out of her home. But she needed a few hundred dollars to expand her business. DSCA provided first one and then a second loan. This woman now has a bank account and expanded income. She has also become a Christian and chose the name "Angela" for herself at her baptism.

The fifth major area of DSCA is spiritual formation, worship, and church planting. In fact, describing this area as a separate component is only partly right, because prayer, Bible study, and witness to Christ flow through every program. All of the different ministries begin each day with a devotional time, including prayer to Christ. There is a monthly all-day prayer meeting for staff. Trained evangelists visit the homes of families involved in the various programs, praying for the sick, teaching the Bible, and sharing the Gospel.

Mrs. Violet Eltham is one of the evangelists. She used to attend both Muslim mosques and Hindu temples. But one day she had a powerful encounter with Jesus Christ. After crying for two days about her sins, she heard a voice saying, "I have forgiven your sins; don't do it again."

Mrs. Etham is now a paid evangelist with DSCA. She visits the sick in their homes, singing and praying for them. She used to live in a different area some distance from where she did visitation, but then one day someone said to her, "You come here, you speak, you go away, but you don't know our troubles. If you come and stay with us and preach to us, then we'll say we can manage." So she decided to move! Now she visits fifteen or twenty homes a day.

The Reverend John Santosh is senior pastor of the Divya Shanthi Community Church and the head of DSCA's religious activities. The Reverend Santosh's department is linked to all the different programs through morning devotions that every program conducts. (They all study the same biblical passage.) His pastoral staff of twenty-five do home visitation.

The church is growing. DSCA started three new community

churches in 1992 with Sunday services in Tamil, Kanada, and English.

Reluctantly, DSCA has found it necessary to establish a new Fellowship of Community Churches. Both at St. John's and then at Lingarajapuram until 1988, Vinay pastored a congregation of the church of South India. The Divya Shanthi CSI church in Lingarajapuram was the center of DSCA's activities. But when Vinay transferred to another congregation in 1988, the Divya Shanthi congregation slowly turned inward. It became increasingly middle class and less concerned to evangelize and nurture poor people. It preferred to focus on traditional liturgy and bureaucratic committee structures.

Eventually DSCA felt compelled to organize a new circle of community churches more suitable to the growing numbers of poor believers coming to Christ from other faiths through DSCA's multiple ministries. By early 1993, there were five DSCA congregations in the new Fellowship of Community Churches.

Vinay and Colleen have developed a unique model for integrating evangelism and social transformation in a context of religious pluralism. In Lingarajapuram where DSCA started, fifty percent of the people are Hindus; forty percent are Muslims; and ten percent are Christians.

Vinay and Colleen wanted to lead people to Christ and plant churches. But they also wanted to transform the socio economic life of the whole community. So they decided to develop a core leadership team of devout Christians and then let the rest of the staff reflect the religious diversity of the community. All programs are open to everyone regardless of religious beliefs.

DSCA treats the religious commitments of non-Christians with great respect and is very careful not to push for hasty conversion and baptism. Vinay believes that if they had stressed immediate conversion and baptism, they would have been quickly marginalized. Instead, by refusing to be in a hurry for conversion, they have been able to win everyone's trust and bring social change to the whole community.

But DSCA does not hide its Christian convictions. Every program begins each day with devotions and prayer to Christ. Hindu, Muslim, and Christian staff attend the Bible studies and prayer meetings. "We had no problem," Vinay said, "working with Hindus and Muslims to bring about social change, without ever compromising that we were evangelical Christians who shared the Gospel and invited people to accept Christ."

This is not syncretism. DSCA does not say to Muslims and Hindus: "You pray to your God, and we'll pray to our God." Instead, Vinay explains, "We say, no, we pray to Christ here. We believe that Christ is the one true God." Many of the Muslims and Hindus become secret believers in Christ well before they take the socially costly and sometimes dangerous step of baptism.

DSCA's response to a tragedy on September 13, 1987, illustrates their approach. In the middle of the night, the city dumped twenty-three hundred very poor families from a Bangalore slum into the middle of Lingarajapuram. DSCA responded immediately with food and temporary housing. Sixty percent of the adults were street vendors who lost their little bit of working capital in the disruption. So DSCA developed a revolving-credit program that provided about thirty dollars of working capital per businessperson so they could restart their tiny businesses. A school, a health program, and vocational training programs followed.

From the beginning, DSCA worked with the leaders of this largely Hindu and Muslim group. When they said their first priority was to replace the Muslim mosque and Hindu temple they had lost, DSCA helped them find the land.

Adult education became one of the central programs. Eventually eight hundred adults participated. The Bible was the textbook used for instruction. Two senior evangelists from DSCA trained leaders (mostly Hindus and Muslims) to lead the adult education groups, which included prayer as well as Bible study. Ninety percent of the eight hundred people who went through the adult-education program were Hindu and Muslim. By the end of two years, however, fifty percent reported that Christ had become real to them. Thirty adults (twenty of them from Hindu and Muslim backgrounds) became full-time employees in DSCA's various programs with the community. All of those leaders now worship Christ alone.[3] They attend the three local Sunday-worship centers that have now become community churches. Most of those who worship at these community centers are unbaptized believers. It continues to be a matter of prayer and debate concerning the timing of their baptism.

Not everyone becomes a Christian. Some Muslims and Hindus, in fact, become better Muslims and Hindus. New churches do not spring up rapidly at the beginning, but the long-term result is both major social transformation in the total community as well as steady church growth.

Vinay labels their approach an "evangelism of the way." They live among the poor, share their resources with everyone, respect the religious beliefs of all, yet constantly make it clear that everything they do is done in the name of Jesus Christ. And when the time is ripe, they invite people to accept Christ, baptize, and plant churches.

What are the critical factors that have made possible this highly successful ministry? Most important, of course, is the presence and activity of the Lord and Vinay's and Colleen's single-minded desire to place Christ at the very center of their lives.

Also crucial is their willingness to follow the pattern of the Incarnate One and live among the poor, sharing their agony and struggle. A guiding theological conviction in all of Vinay's work is that God has a special concern for the poor. So Vinay, and Colleen "adopted" Lingarajapuram with all its pain and brokenness.

And they listened to its people. At the beginning, they did careful surveys to identify the needs of the community. But the way they did their survey made a significant theological point. Vinay has been called a "theologian of dignity"—a theologian who seeks to respect and strengthen the dignity of the poorest.[4] So in their surveys, they ask not what people *need*, but what they *hope* for!

Vinay and Colleen believe that building genuine partnership is a central key to working with the poor. How do they do that as educated people from business families? Colleen calls it "moving from the chair to the floor." Most of the slum dwellers they serve have no chairs in their tiny houses. So when Colleen and Vinay visit, they sit on the floor as everyone else does. "That is the heart of incarnating the Gospel," Vinay says. It certainly builds authentic partnership.

Strong indigenous Christian leadership and international

partnership have both been essential elements in DSCA's success. Vinay and Colleen gathered around them a core leadership group of about twenty-five dedicated Christians that work in the programs and serve on DSCA's board. Program managers receive wide freedom to develop their areas. The long-standing partnership of respect and trust with a few donor agencies, especially Tear Fund (Holland) and Mrs. Anky Rookmaaker, has provided an essential financial base.

There is no formula, however, that can guarantee the success God has given Vinay and Colleen. It flows from a mysterious mix of costly discipleship, deep faith, unusual ability, and divine grace.

To ignore the presence and power of God at work in DSCA would be very wrong. It would also be inaccurate to overlook the fact that the unusual faith and giftedness of Colleen and Vinay have contributed significantly to DSCA's success. Colleen combines gentle compassion and seasoned wisdom with blazing courage and disciplined dedication.

Vinay brings the same deep faith combined with a photographic memory and a brilliant mind. Simply to have accomplished, in the past twenty years, what they have done in evangelism and community development in Bangalore would be unusual. But Vinay has, at the same time, become a prominent theological spokesman for Two-Third World Christians, an international leader in both ecumenical and evangelical circles, and a key organizer of important international conferences, movements and organizations.[5] He now serves as the Executive Director of the International Fellowship of Evangelical Missions Theologians.

Two institutions Vinay founded merit special attention: TAFTEE and the EFICOR training program.

Today the Association for Theological Education by Extension (TAFTEE) offers correspondence courses to over seven thousand people all across India. In 1970, when he was only twenty-eight years old, Vinay started TAFTEE in order to equip lay Christians who would never be able to attend a theological school. The course that he and Chris Sugden wrote on Poverty and Development is now used in eighty countries. The certificate, diploma, and degree-level courses TAFTEE now offers in nine different languages have strengthened the faith and ministry of literally thousands of Christians all across the Indian subcontinent.

In 1977, Vinay founded a program to train development workers for the Evangelical Fellowship of India's relief and development arm (EFICOR). This three-month program has trained five-hundred-fifty community-development workers who now work throughout India and South Asia. These community workers combine development work with a passionate commitment to evangelism. Placed in rural and tribal communities across India, they have developed models of mission for indigenous missionary societies.

That Vinay could do all this and more at the same time that he and Colleen developed the rapidly growing ministries at DSCA reflects both special ability and unusual divine blessing.

Not all has been joy and ecstasy, to be sure. Danger, anxiety, and failure have all been present. The first church that Vinay and Colleen built at Lingarajapuram not only turned inward and lost the vision. Its new pastor even went to court to try to force DSCA to stop using its facilities.

Dedicated leadership by parents also demands much from children. Sometimes the Samuel children have missed Dad, who was in another part of the globe, or Mom, who was caring for someone else's neglected son or daughter. Living in the slum of Lingarajapuram was not always easy. The youngest child, Mark, may have permanent health problems because of the poor water at Lingarajapuram. Mark contracted typhoid fever and then developed rheumatoid arthritis.

Nevertheless, it also involved much joy. One of the best Christmases the family ever had, Vinay told me, happened when they decided to share in an unusual way with their very poor neighbors in Lingarajapuram. Each family member, including the children, picked one other person and shared a major part of their Christmas budget with that person. That meant that thirteen-year-old Mark did not get the bicycle he badly wanted. They also chose one neighbor family and gave that family the money they needed so that another family could experience the joy and dignity of throwing a Christmas party for *their* friends.

As a middle-class family living in the slums, they struggled to develop a faithful lifestyle. "Can you live with integrity as a Christian," Vinay wonders, "with all that you have, when those next door to you with whom you are sharing the Gospel are poor—really abjectly poor?" The children attended middle-class schools, but they gave up some of the things (like a bicycle for a thirteen-year-old boy) that they would have otherwise enjoyed. They tried to develop what Vinay calls a "sharing lifestyle."

God has blessed the Samuels' faith and sacrifice. DSCA is enjoying an ever-widening impact. The Fellowship of Community Churches is growing. They have recently opened new boarding homes in two other cities. They plan to start a new infirmary that will provide cheaper medical care for people who otherwise would need to go to the local hospital. They are well on the way to launching a major new housing project that will build twenty-five hundred new houses. The Oxford Center for Mission Studies, which Vinay helped organize, now offers graduate degrees nurturing the kind of wholistic mission Vinay and Colleen have developed.

The story of Colleen and Vinay is a story of faith, courage, and obedience. And at its center is Jesus Christ. Colleen speaks for both: "The only motivation has been and will always be the person of Jesus Christ."

Through the ministry of Vinay and Colleen, Jesus transforms broken people—even powerful prostitutes. Everybody in their area knew about Lola.[6] She was the leader of all the prostitutes in a large section of Bangalore. She could swing elections with the twenty thousand votes she controlled. Nobody tangled with Lola.

One day, without any warning, Lola walked in and sat down in the back row at church. A wave of terror swept the congregation, but Colleen walked over, gave her a big hug, and welcomed her to the service.

Lola began to attend regularly. Six months later she accepted Christ. Change was not instantaneous, but by the end of two years, her life had been beautifully transformed. She asked for baptism.

Vinay faced a dangerous decision. He knew that if he proceeded to baptize this famous Muslim woman, there would be religious riots. Their whole work might be destroyed.

So Vinay went to talk to the local Muslim leader. "My dear friend," he told the Imam. "You know this lady. She wants to be baptized. I want you to dissuade her from becoming a Christian. Take a whole month." The Imam was surprised, but he agreed to try.

Three days later, he was back. "Quite frankly," he said, "I don't think I can do anything. She is so much better off with you. She has changed so much." When Vinay asked him if he minded if Lola were baptized, he answered: "You can do what you like." Vinay baptized Lola. No riots occurred. Today she is a full-time evangelist.

---

1 Unless otherwise indicated, quotes are from personal interviews.

2 Vinay and Colleen Samuel, "Rebuilding Families: A Priority for Wholistic Mission," *Transformation*, July–September 1993, 7.

3 See Vinay Samuel, "India: Evangelism Among the Urban Poor," in Christopher Wright and Christopher Sugden, eds., *One Gospel-Many Clothes: Anglicans and the Decade of Evangelism* (Oxford: Regnum Books, 1990), 80–85.

4 See Christopher Sugden's dissertation on Vinay Samuel's work and theology: *A Critical and Comparative Study. . . of Wayan Mastra . . . and Vinay Samuel . . .* (Unpublished dissertation, Westminster College, Oxford, 1987), especially 217ff.

5 The following are some of his many writings:

Vinay Samuel and Albrecht Hauser, eds., *Proclaiming Christ in Christ's Way: Studies in Integral Evangelism* (Oxford: Regnum, 1989); Vinay Samuel and Christopher Sugden, *Lambeth: A View from the Two-Thirds World* (London: SPCK, 1989); Vinay Samuel and Christopher Sugden, *Christian Mission in the Eighties: A Third World Perspective* (Partnership Booklet, No. 2; Bangalore: Partnership in Mission-Asia, 1981); Vinay Samuel and Christopher Sugden, "Evangelism and Social Responsibility: A Biblical Study on Priorities" in Bruce J. Nicholls, ed., *In Word and Deed* (Grand Rapids: Eerdmans, 1985), pp. 189–214; Vinay Samuel and Christopher Sugden, *Evangelism and the Poor: A Third World Study Guide* (Revised Edition; Oxford: Regnum Books, 1983); Vinay Samuel and Christopher Sugden, eds., *The Church in Response to Human Need* (Grand Rapids: Eerdmans; Oxford: Regnum, 1987); Vinay Samuel and Christopher Sugden, *A.D. 2000 and Beyond: A Mission Agenda* (Oxford: Regnum, 1991); Vinay Samuel has also written numerous articles for *Transformation*, which he co-edits.

6 I have changed the name.

4

A Fudge-Ripple Partnership in Inner-City Chicago

What would happen in our society if racial reconciliation became an evangelical agenda as important as abortion?

Raleigh Washington and Glen Kehrein

Where would you go if you were looking for two people to pioneer ministry in one of the toughest inner-city neighborhoods of Chicago? Probably not to Ripon, Wisconsin, a little overwhelmingly white town in rural Wisconsin where the Republican Party began. And probably not to the upper levels of the U.S. army where a highly successful black lieutenant colonel enjoyed his affluent lifestyle and never intended to return to the ghetto he had escaped.

But that's where God went for the two central leaders of one of Chicago's most dynamic wholistic ministries.

Today Raleigh Washington and Glen Kehrein lead a growing church and a huge community center that serves about thirty thousand people every year.[1] Circle Urban Ministries, which Glen oversees as Executive Director, rehabilitates old houses, trains inner-city folk for jobs, starts small businesses, runs a medical clinic and a legal clinic. It is a multimillion-dollar cluster of community-development programs. Pastor Raleigh leads Rock of Our Salvation Evangelical Free Church, an interracial congregation with a weekly attendance of about three hundred-fifty that meets in the gymnasium of the community center. Raleigh's and Glen's close relationship of unusual trust and mutual partnership is the core of this amazing model of racial reconciliation and intertwined evangelism and social transformation.

Today, as you look at Rock/Circle's successful ministries, it might be easy to miss the pain, frustration, and failure that have been central to their birth and growth. These large, growing programs did not happen easily. They blossomed out of soil filled with struggle and agony.

The story of the community center starts with Glen Kehrein, who grew up in a devout evangelical home in the small white town of Ripon, Wisconsin. Ripon had no black residents. In fact, Glen never ever spoke to an African-American until he was an adult. Things were not much different at Moody Bible Institute when Glen began his studies in 1966. Interracial dating was forbidden.

Glen, however, discovered an astonishing new world in inner-city Chicago each day as he led an evangelistic youth club in a poor area near Moody. He also listened to the pain of a few fellow black students. Slowly, Glen began to struggle with the racism he had unconsciously adopted while growing up. When Chicago exploded after Martin Luther King's assassination in April 1968, Glen sensed a growing call to the city. After graduation Glen married his high-school sweetheart, Lonni. Fortunately, Lonni shared his vision. Together, as urban pioneers, they dreamed of transforming Chicago.

Their first effort ended with a murder. They began a youth club for black inner-city kids, but when a key leader was killed in a hold-up, the sponsoring church lost interest.

In 1971, Glen and Lonni discovered Circle Church on Chicago's West Side. Already famous in evangelical circles as an early interracial congregation,[2] Circle encouraged Glen to start a community center. John Perkins had inspired them with his vision of wholistic ministry and church planting led by people who relocate in the community of need. So Glen and Lonni moved in June 1973 into a transitional neighborhood in the Austin section of Chicago. In 1960, no blacks lived in Austin. By 1970, Austin was seventy percent black. Ten years later, the transition was complete. Glen, Lonni, and a few others from Circle developed a counseling program, a legal-aid clinic, and a youth program. But just as this new ministry, called Circle Community Center, began to take off, the sponsoring church flew apart in blazing racial conflict.

Somehow Circle Community Center continued to develop with the support from the white folk who remained in Circle

Church, but all the black members of Circle left. It was awkward and embarrassing to be ministering to an overwhelmingly black community without any black leaders. As Executive Director, Glen prayed and searched for black colleagues. One helpful partnership ended disastrously when Glen challenged his black colleague for having walked out on his wife. Furious, the man threw Glen across the room and nearly broke his arm. Glen began to despair of the possibility of genuine, deep, black-white partnership in his lifetime. Maybe, he hoped, his children could do better.

In spite of all this, the community center's programs continued to grow—at least in numbers. The official connection with what was left of Circle Church ended in 1980, but Circle Community Center kept expanding. They developed a medical clinic and started to rehab old housing. By 1983, they had a full-time staff of twenty people. On the surface, things looked good, but Glen was almost ready to give up. His heart ached over the failure to find black partners in ministry. He also knew they were not really faithful to the original vision that combined evangelism and social transformation.

Circle Community was doing precious little evangelism. They were wholistic only in principle. Glen now realizes that when they started they were "anti-establishment children of the sixties" who looked down on people passing out tracts on street corners. They were evangelicals who theoretically believed in evangelism but they considered many popular evangelistic techniques insensitive and harmful. They preferred "relational evangelism": "We'll act out the Gospel. Demonstrate it. People will see what we do and ask us why we do it." "The only problem," Glen now admits, is that "not many people asked why we were doing what we were doing."[3]

Slowly Glen began to realize that in spite of all their programs, they were not making a long-term difference in people's lives. "What is the measuring rod for what we do?" Glen asked himself. "Is it the number of buildings we rehab? Is it the number of people we serve? The reality is that none of that is an important end. The end is how many lives we see changed. And in the first ten years of our ministry, we didn't see very many lives changed."[4] They had come dangerously close to becoming a typical Christian social agency without any genuine evangelistic component.

Fortunately, God was preparing an answer to Glen's problems. God was dramatically working in the life of a gifted, successful lieutenant colonel in the U.S. army, Raleigh Washington. Raleigh was born in 1938 into a very poor black family headed by a single mom living in the projects of Jacksonville, Florida. The segregated schools Raleigh attended through college were often very poor. But Raleigh was determined and competitive. During his first year at (all-black) Florida A & M he could not even afford to buy any books. So he studied late at night using his friends' books after they had finished. Fortunately, he won a baseball scholarship for the next three years that covered all his expenses. In fact, he was so good that the Chicago Cubs offered him a contract, but Raleigh preferred to complete his college degree.

College ROTC led Raleigh to a highly successful military career. After graduation, he joined fifty-nine other second lieutenants for special training. All the rest were white. Raleigh was determined to succeed. Hard work, a competitive spirit, and extraordinary natural ability produced one promotion after another. Raleigh performed brilliantly and moved rapidly up the military ladder. By 1977, he was a lieutenant colonel in charge of the San Juan District Recruiting Command—the first black officer to obtain such a position.

But trouble was brewing behind the scenes. Raleigh had competed with many white colleagues for positions. And this black man had won! He had disciplined and fired white officers. Losing to a black man made them furious. Trumped-up charges based on racial prejudice eventually led to a trial. There was no basis for prosecution and no evidence, but the generals on Raleigh's review board were clearly prejudiced. Three days before he could have retired with a full pension, the army gave Raleigh a painful choice: He could retire with full benefits "in lieu" of being discharged. But that meant quietly admitting that he was guilty. He refused. So the army threw him out on July 29, 1980, one day before he would have retired with full benefits after a twenty-year career.

Fortunately, Raleigh and his wife, Paulette, had been marvelously converted just three years earlier. Sensing a call to preach, Raleigh enrolled in Trinity Evangelical Divinity School in Deerfield, Illinois. It was tough. Their annual income dropped from forty-eight thousand dollars to four thousand. And they had five children. Somehow they survived.

At seminary, Raleigh developed a passion for evangelism and church planting. He dreamed of starting a church back home in Florida. But God had other plans.

A seminary professor at Trinity realized that Glen Kehrein's Circle Community Center might be an ideal place to start a church. So he took Raleigh and Paulette to Austin. Both Raleigh and Glen were cautious. Glen wondered if Raleigh represented just one more painful failure at black-white cooperation. Raleigh, for his part, had no intention of living in the Austin ghetto.

South Austin is a tough neighborhood. Four gangs operate in the area. Two years ago, just two blocks from the community center, two hundred FBI and DEA agents swooped in for the largest drug bust in Chicago's history. Only six percent of the students read at their proper grade level. Over sixty percent of the students drop out before completing high school. Fifty-eight percent of the households are headed by women. Thirty-two percent of the people are on welfare.

That's precisely the kind of neighborhood in which Raleigh had grown up—and escaped! As a successful military officer he had become accustomed to an affluent lifestyle. He had no interest in returning to an impoverished black ghetto. Raleigh wanted to plant a church in some nice, integrated, middle-class neighborhood.

God, however, kept opening doors in the inner city. Glen offered to let Raleigh start a church using space in the community center. His wife, Paulette, seemed eager to move to the inner city. A Jewish lawyer offered the down payment for a house near the community center. Raleigh was also impressed by Glen's and Lonni's commitment to the poor. If they could live in the inner city, so could he. Finally Raleigh told his wife: "If people like us don't return to bring God's hope and resources back into the ghetto, how are we going to facilitate change?"[5]

So in 1983 the Washington family moved to South Austin, and

Raleigh started to share the Gospel with neighborhood people who came to Circle Community Center.

At first the professional staff at the center resisted, or at least were uneasy about, Raleigh's evangelistic programs. For his part, Raleigh was appalled that these socially concerned Christians seemed far more interested in caring for peoples' physical needs than in leading them to Jesus Christ. But Glen reminded everyone that evangelism had been part of their original vision. Glen and Lonni joined Raleigh's new church. Glen also recommended that Raleigh be elected chair of the board of the community center. Solid trust and mutual partnership began to take root.

So did Pastor Washington's new congregation. He offered to be a volunteer chaplain at the community center and began counseling those who mentioned spiritual needs. He also did door-to-door evangelism in the neighborhood. When he identified himself as the pastor of the church that was meeting at Circle Urban Ministries (they changed the name in 1985), the people gladly invited him in. They also accepted Christ. In the early years, most of the new members at Rock Church were converts whose first contact came through the community center. Raleigh's enthusiasm for evangelism, his solid biblical preaching, and the link with the center produced steady church growth.

Over the first five years of Raleigh's presence, his evangelistic passion changed the community center dramatically. Raleigh helped Glen see that unless the doctors, lawyers, and educators at Circle all cared about evangelism, it simply would not happen. So Glen added "a heart for evangelism" to his list of qualifications for most positions at the center. "You can't legislate it," Glen says. "It comes out of the hearts of people." During these five years, there was almost a complete turnover of staff. By the end, almost all were enthusiastic about the new centrality of evangelism that Raleigh encouraged.

By 1993, ten years after Raleigh arrived, Rock/Circle had become one closely intertwined network of ministries with the church and community center tightly interrelated. Raleigh chairs the board of the community center. For the first nine years, Glen chaired the board of elders of the church. Three of the church's pastors also work as chaplains in the community center. The church meets in the gymnasium of the center.

Both are growing. About three hundred-fifty people attend church on a typical Sunday. Seventy percent are black and thirty percent are white. For 1994, the budget of Circle Urban Ministries (CUM) was two million dollars. And that does not include the operations of the medical clinic or the affiliated organization that owns and rents three hundred units of low income housing.

CUM's programs fall into eight basic areas: emergency care, housing, job training and small business development, education, youth, medical work, legal assistance, and chaplaincy.

Emergency care. In 1992, CUM touched the lives of ten thousand people with emergency care—temporary housing, food, and clothing.

Marie Hall was desperate when she called CUM's emergency housing service in 1985. She had lost her job and was one day away from being thrown out on the street. Every emergency-housing shelter she called refused to allow her thirteen-year-old son to come with her and her daughter, and she desperately wanted to keep her family together.

Then she learned of CUM's unusual emergency housing. Unlike most programs for the homeless, CUM houses people in apartments precisely so families can stay together. CUM had an apartment for Marie within a day. CUM's chaplains and caseworkers met regularly with Marie. Her modest rent went into an escrow account so she would have a security deposit for her next apartment. Today Marie is off welfare. She works full-time at CUM and attends Rock Church.

With eighteen well-furnished apartments, CUM serves one hundred families a year. CUM's family service workers visit all residents helping with whatever needs they have—rescheduling debts, improving their budgeting, finding a job and an apartment. CUM's chaplains also visit to talk about spiritual needs and invite residents to Rock Church.

Once, fairly early in CUM's work in emergency housing, a city administrator came by. She was so impressed with their unique approach that she invited them to apply for city funds to expand their operations. Glen's response was to show her a video that explicitly described how evangelism was part of their program. She immediately raised the question of separation of church and state. Glen replied that city funding was attractive but "not at the expense of what makes the program go." She finally agreed to fund CUM as long as they did not require church attendance. (They don't!) The city knows that church-related programs like CUM's are far cheaper and more effective than city-run programs, so they give CUM a large margin of freedom to run their programs the way they want to. CUM's approach is to be clear about what they do and then refuse funding that would prevent their ministering to the whole person.

CUM also provides emergency food and clothing. In a typical month, six hundred to one thousand people receive twenty thousand pounds of food donated by churches and the Greater Chicago Depository (a food bank). Their resale shop provides inexpensive quality clothes. Charging a small fee prevents abuse and provides dignity.

Housing. CUM began rehabbing housing in 1981 to save the neighborhood. Ruthless landlords often ignored tax bills and refused to make renovations. When they had milked as much money as possible from their deteriorating apartments, they abandoned the run-down buildings to city tax collectors. Bulldozers demolished three thousand apartments in Austin alone in the eight years before CUM started rehabbing in 1981.

Since then, CUM has restored three-hundred-sixty lower-income apartment units. CUM's wholly owned subsidiary, Circle Urban Development Corporation, owns and rents three hundred of these. Various kinds of subsidies (often federal financing through HUD) enables CUM to rent its apartments at affordable rates.

Only recently has CUM begun to work at home ownership. But they acquired a number of vacant lots in 1992. Soon, they hope, they can build and sell modestly priced individual houses to their Austin neighbors.

Job training and small business development. Both good jobs and well-prepared workers are often hard to find in South Austin. Businesses have moved to the suburbs or Mexico. Ex-offenders, former drug addicts, and long-time welfare recipients often find it difficult to meet the demands of a regular job. So in 1987, CUM started an employment service. By 1992, with support from World Vision, CUM offered job readiness training to two hundred low-income or difficult-to-employ men and women.

The best kind of training, they have discovered, is "reality based." That means that CUM provides a genuine work environment where people learn real job skills and discipline. For example, they discovered that a large switch company was throwing away used switches that could be disassembled, repaired, and reused. So CUM got a large contract to sort and rebuild the switches. CUM's job trainees enjoyed excellent work experience, and the switch company saved a large amount of money. Unfortunately, the company realized they could save even more dollars if they had the same work done in Mexico where labor is much cheaper. So CUM lost this lucrative contract. (That's one reason there is poverty in our inner cities.)

More and more, CUM is switching from job placement to job creation and small-business development. Circle Pallet Company, which started in 1991, is a great example. A large local cosmetics firm, Helene Curtis, uses tens of thousands of wooden pallets each month to ship its products. Many are damaged. Circle Pallet sorts the used pallets, repairs the damaged ones, and returns them all to the cosmetic firm. In the first three months of operation, they did over thirty thousand pallets and made a profit. Today there are twelve full-time employees working at this successful business. In 1993, Circle Pallet made a net profit of fifty thousand dollars.

From the beginning, one central goal was to empower black people in Austin to become entrepreneurs. Showen Franklin, a former "Gang-Banger," is one example. Showen came to Christ through Rock/Circle, and is now the General Manager of Circle Pallet. CUM is also exploring the possibility of starting other businesses. They plan to develop three-way partnerships in which a Chicago business person with money and know-how joins with CUM and a neighborhood person from Rock/Circle who will be trained to take over the business eventually.

Education. An educational Summer Camp for kids, tutoring during the academic year for school children, and a GED program for adults are three ways that CUM empowers people through education.

Every year about one hundred inner-city kids (ages six to thirteen) attend CUM's Camp Gideon. Training in math and reading are intertwined with recreation, fun, and games. During the academic year, Christian volunteers tutor eighty school-age children. Devotional times for the children and evangelistic events for their parents are central parts of the tutoring program.

The GED program is a successful program, partially founded by the city, that enables adults to study for their high-school diploma. Each year CUM runs six eight-week terms. Eighty to ninety adults enroll each term. Many begin at grade-school levels in reading and math. Not nearly everyone receives the high-school degree, but everyone improves his or her skills.

Meg Cox, the GED coordinator until recently, explained how CUM's spiritual concerns inform the program. There is no Bible class in the curriculum, since the city pays for the four teachers through Wright College, which does most of Chicago's adult education. But CUM's program retains students better than most, so they have considerable freedom. CUM recommends Christian teachers, who are usually accepted. These teachers openly discuss their faith. Once a week a voluntary prayer meeting takes place after class. CUM hires and pays the coordinator, so the leader of the program is committed to their Christian vision and approach.

Youth development. Ed Johnson is the youth chaplain and youth director at CUM and the youth minister at Rock Church. He is developing a very intensive program designed to help community youth move toward personal and spiritual development. An after-school program, a recreation program, and a jobs program all help prepare community youth to become Circle's next generation of leaders.

Medical care and counseling. The story of Circle's medical center illustrates the complexity and difficulty of developing a genuinely wholistic program. Circle's medical program began in the early years of the ministry. By the time Pastor Raleigh arrived in 1983, it was a large, successful clinic called Circle Family Care, affiliated with the community center but accountable to its own board.

Not everyone at CFC was enthusiastic about Raleigh's new style of implicit evangelism. Some doctors were very supportive; others preferred to do their witnessing with their hands. When CFC accepted a large federal grant without adequately protecting (at least according to Rock/Circle leaders) their ability to be openly evangelistic, the community center and the clinic decided to dissolve their affiliation. For a time, it looked as if CUM would set up its own totally separate program.

Fortunately, by early 1994, they worked out a happy compromise. By then, CFC had grown to a point where it was running several medical centers in addition to the one housed at CUM. So CFC agreed to let CUM name the medical director (and through him the rest of the staff) for the clinic at CUM. CFC handles administrative matters but gives the medical center at CUM freedom to develop its own special character. As a result, that clinic continues with the wholistic approach of Rock/Circle and the doctors who enthusiastically share that approach. They deal just as directly with spiritual needs as with medical ones. And they are growing. They expect to triple their medical program in the near future to a patient load of approximately ten thousand family units.

Legal aid. CUM runs one of the two legal-aid clinics that serve the poor on the West Side of Chicago where a million people live. The three full-time lawyers (supported by scores of downtown attorneys who donate time) listen daily to desperate people whose lives are in crisis. Frequently, other programs refer people. When Meg Cox, head of the GED program, discovered that one of her students was being abused, she was grateful to be able to send her to a sympathetic lawyer in the legal-aid clinic. Legal fees are nominal. Each year, the legal clinic opens six hundred new cases.

Wanda Caldwell's story shows how these programs work together to transform broken lives. Wanda first came to Rock/Circle in 1983. She was single, pregnant, only seventeen, and so scared that she tried to commit suicide. Counselors at CUM helped her through that crisis. A year later, after drugs and wild parties, she almost died from a ruptured stomach. Dr. Beran at the medical clinic prayed with her just before her surgery. But she returned to drugs and a wild life as a successful rock soloist.

At the height of her success, her life was in chaos. She used drugs regularly and often drank herself senseless. For twelve years she drove a car without a driver's license. She had all her bills (phone, gas, and so forth) in different names and was behind on all of them. She collected welfare even though she was paid fairly well for her music. Her boyfriend was trying to get her hooked on cocaine.

Through all these years, she attended different churches. But they never satisfied—or changed—her. At a moment of deep despair, her mom told her about the church called Rock that met in the gym. Desperate, she decided to attend.

She arrived with her wild hairstyle and wild clothes. Her first surprise was to meet Dr. Beran, the doctor who had prayed with her before surgery. The love and warmth she felt on that first visit from the members of Rock Church overwhelmed her. "It was like the Spirit of the Lord engulfed me and hugged me." She decided to attend regularly.

Wanda found people at Rock/Circle ready to walk with her through her many problems. The medical clinic provided medical care and counseling for her and her children. Years of ignoring bills meant that she was close to going to jail. The legal clinic helped, and the bill collectors were patient when she confessed. She got a driver's license.

Paul Grant, music minister at Rock Church and full-time chaplain at CUM, gently yet firmly walked with her through the painful, drastic changes she needed to make. Sometimes she wanted to throw things at Paul for his tough love, but he and others persisted. "They really had some patience," Wanda says. "If they had given up, I would probably still be out on the street, just as wild as anything that's out there right now. But they kept calling, kept holding on to me, kept hugging me, kept telling me that they loved me. I didn't think I was worthy to be loved that much."

Today, Wanda and her happy children tell others about Christ. Recently she visited an old friend in the hospital. In earlier days, they used to "hang" together on the street. Then a bullet paralyzed him from the waist down. When she told him her story, her friend also accepted Christ.

God—and God's faithful people—have transformed Wanda.

She is off welfare. She works at Trinity Evangelical Divinity School to support her children. And she uses her gift of song to sing for the Lord. "I've come a long way," Wanda says.

Evangelism. Circle Urban Ministries is strikingly different from many church-related social programs. Why? Because CUM brings evangelism into the center of its work. In all their programs, they have staff eager to share Christ. CUM also hires chaplains who focus on evangelism. And together with Rock Church, they hold a week-long series of evangelistic events every summer called Harvest.

CUM hired its first chaplain in 1985 as a conscious effort to make evangelism more open and central in the work of the community center. Today CUM has two full-time and one part-time chaplains. Several work part-time as pastors for the church and part-time as chaplains for the community center.

Preaching to people waiting for food and clothing in emergency care often produces a dramatic response. Raleigh's brother, Lincoln Washington, explains why. Many of the people need food because they have used their monthly check on drugs. "They're feeling down. They've been hurting their families. You find guilty people," Lincoln says. Many hands go up when Lincoln preaches and invites people to accept Christ's forgiving love. During one month, seventy-eight people responded.

Follow-up, however, is hard. People are transient. Not nearly all end up in church, but some do. Lincoln estimates that of those seventy-eight from that one month, four or five are now in Rock Church.

The chaplains also follow up people referred to them by the staff. If a doctor senses a spiritual need, the doctor encourages the person to go see a chaplain or asks if the person would like a follow-up visit at home. The double impact of a doctor's taking time to pray with the patient and then a chaplain's following up that contact is powerful.

Mrs. La Verne Green works especially with women in CUM's apartment buildings. Starting with some names from other CUM staff, she began to knock on doors. She had a easy answer when people called out, "Who's out there, the Jehovah's Witnesses?" Doors quickly opened when she replied, "No, this is Circle Urban

Ministries." She has eight Bible studies going in different apartment buildings.

I will always associate Rock/Circle's annual Harvest week with a telephone conversation I had with Raleigh Washington in the late summer of 1991. I had called him to discuss serving on a board. Initially, however, Raleigh was too exited to talk about that. He wanted to tell me about the eight hundred-twenty-two people who had responded to the Gospel the previous week in their Harvest programs.

During Harvest, Rock/Circle pitches a tent in a nearby vacant lot and holds evangelistic meetings. The week culminates with a huge Saturday barbecue for about seven hundred-fifty neighborhood people. At the end, Raleigh preaches. In 1993, two hundred-fifty people made commitments to Christ.

Follow-up here is just as tough as in emergency care. People are constantly moving. Follow-up committees find it hard to track people down. This problem prompted a change in Harvest '93. The Harvest tent stayed up for an extra week so they could conduct special services for new believers. Then they assigned each new Christian to a ten-week discipleship group.

It is precisely the inseparable interconnections of Rock Church and the community center that make their evangelism so powerful. Glen acknowledges that before Raleigh started the church and prompted more evangelism, "few lives were permanently changed for the better."[6] Today dozens and dozens of people are in Rock Church (as well as other churches) because of Rock/Circle's blend of evangelism and social transformation. "I've come to believe," Glen says, "that it's practically impossible to do effective holistic ministry apart from the church."[7] In fact, Glen adds, "if someone were to offer me a million dollars to direct an urban ministry somewhere else that lacked the support network we have here through the church, I wouldn't have to think twice before turning it down."[8]

Rock of Our Salvation Evangelical Free Church is one of only a very small number of successful multi-racial churches. Pastor Raleigh believes that racial reconciliation is central to the Gospel. St. Paul, he insists, preached "a gospel of reconciliation not only between men and God, but between cultures and peoples.

Homogeneous churches," he adds, "may be easier but they are not God's intent."[9]

But it is one thing to preach racial reconciliation, another thing to practice it. Both happen at Rock Church. And the very special relationship of trust and partnership between Raleigh and Glen is one of the primary reasons. Both are strong, vigorous men. They do not hide their differences or sidestep conflict, but they feel called to racial reconciliation—and they love each other very deeply. The genuine partnership, deep respect, and mutual submission they model permeates the whole church.

Even so, Rock Church has to work hard at avoiding serious racial tension. Four times a year, they hold a "Fudge-Ripple" process. Pastor Washington meets alone with all the black members of the church in their "chocolate" session. Then he meets with just the white members for a "vanilla" discussion. In both cases he encourages open sharing of feelings and concerns. Finally they come together to deal directly and honestly with differences in a combined "fudge-ripple dialogue." The meetings are often lively. But these quarterly fudge-ripple Sundays help bind together this congregation which is seventy percent black and thirty percent white.

Not all is the way I would like it at Rock Church. I wish the congregation did not have a policy that allows only men to serve as elders or be ordained as pastors. In fact, women actually play central roles at the church. Raleigh's wife, Paulette, is a very gifted evangelist who speaks widely both at Rock Church and around the country. And Glen's wife, Lonni, is the gifted minister of education at Rock Church. But the congregation's rules exclude them from being elders or ordained pastors.

Whatever its shortcomings, however, Rock Church is a wonderful gift to the church in the U.S. In a country where Sunday worship is still the most racially segregated hour of the week, Rock Church stands as a visible sign of success and hope. It also stands as a call to action. In their powerful new book, *Breaking Down Walls*, Raleigh and Glen insist that all Christians are called to work for racial reconciliation. And they ask a haunting question: "What would happen in our society if racial reconciliation became an evangelical agenda as important as abortion?"[10]

The strength that comes from genuine partnership is clear in many aspects of Rock/Circle's life and ministry. The role of suburban and rural volunteers is one example. In the last ten years, over three thousand volunteers, not only from greater Chicago but from Nebraska to Pennsylvania, have donated tens of thousands of hours of labor to Rock/Circle.

The volunteers receive as much as they give. One man with deep-seated racial prejudice felt very hesitant to travel with his church group to Rock/Circle. But the visible demonstration of racial reconciliation that he witnessed at Rock/Circle began to melt his heart. Back home, he wept as he confessed his prejudice and told how the Gospel of reconciliation was transforming his life.

No one story can sum up all the wonderful things God is doing at Rock/Circle. But the story of Cassandra and Showen Franklin comes close.

Cassandra's first contact was with the medical clinic. A single mom with one little child, she felt devastated when Dr. Beran told her she was pregnant again. Should she get an abortion? Dr. Beran encouraged her to talk to one of the clinic's counselors. He even checked to make sure she kept the appointment and sat with her so she would feel more comfortable.

When Dr. Beran and the counselor encouraged her to talk with the chaplain, Paul Grant, she was really frightened. She expected a fire-and-brimstone sermon from some stern preacher. "But I trusted Dr. Beran," Cassandra says. "If he wanted me to go to this session to help me, I wanted to help him help me. So I kept my appointment."

Paul Grant was very different from the person she had imagined. Paul talked gently with her and invited her to Rock Church. "The next week I was there, and I've been coming ever since," Cassandra reports with gratitude. She soon accepted Christ, joined the church, and found a new happiness and peace in her life.

Showen Franklin, however, her boyfriend of six years, was less enthusiastic. All her new talk about these two new friends, Jesus and Paul Grant, made him a bit jealous. It was also clear that she was making major changes that would greatly affect their relationship.

Finally Showen agreed to go to church with Cassandra—partly out of suspicious curiosity and partly because he was intrigued by the changes he saw in his girlfriend. Paul Grant preached that Sunday. And Showen accepted Christ.

That was the beginning of a four-year battle. "I had accepted Christ into my heart," Showen reports, "but I had not made him Lord of my life." For four years Paul Grant patiently prayed for and discipled Showen. Paul's wife, Du Rhonda, did the same with Cassandra.

Eventually, Cassandra and Showen began to think of marriage. After premarital counseling at the center, they married on October 20, 1990—the first Christian marriage in either of their immediate families. "We prayed," Showen says, "that our marriage would be a model of how a Christ-centered marriage would be."[11] They also prayed that their lives would be a testimony to their families, since none of their immediate relatives were Christians. Since then, Showen's nephew, sister, and brother have accepted Christ at Harvest weeks.

Today Cassandra works full-time at the center. And Showen is the General Manager of the Circle Pallet Company, leading CUM's most successful business. They enjoy the happiness of Christian marriage and family, the goodness and dignity of good jobs, and inner peace with God, because Christians at Rock/Circle shared the whole Gospel and then walked with them as God continued the work of transforming them into whole persons.

In fact, Rock/Circle has done that for scores and scores of broken people. John Perkins thinks that more and more large foundations and even government will turn to community-based organizations like Rock/Circle. They should. Nothing else works as well as their combination of loving care for the whole person and the miraculous power of divine grace.

---

1   They have recently told their story in a powerful book called *Breaking Down Walls* (Chicago: Moody, 1993).

2   See David R. Mains, *Full Circle: The Creative Church for Today's Society* (Waco: Word, 1971).

3   Glen Kehrein, "The Church and Wholistic Ministry" in David Caes, ed., *Caring for the Least of These: Serving Christ Among the Poor* (Scottsdale: Herald Press, 1992), 94.

4 Unless otherwise indicated, quotations are from personal interviews with the persons indicated.

5 *Breaking Down Walls*, 216.

6 Ibid., 88.

7 Kehrein, "The Church and Holistic Ministry," in David Caes, ed., *Caring for the Least of These*, 95.

8 Ibid., 96.

9 Quoted in Bob Mueller, "Miracle on Central Street," *Wellspring*, 10.

10 *Breaking Down Walls*, 239.

11 From Showen Franklin's memorial to Paul Grant, who died in a canoe accident in early 1991; see Circle Urban Ministries' May 1991 newsletter.

5

Unleashing a Sleepy, Traditional Congregation: Words, Deeds, and Signs in New Zealand

*I suspect that it is probably easier to drift into a social-concern mode
and to put evangelism on the back burner.*

Brian Hathaway

I first visited Te Atatu Bible Chapel in Auckland, New Zealand in 1986. What I saw in this growing body of believers making solid strides toward modeling Christ's dawning kingdom encouraged and inspired me. White and black, rich and poor, uneducated and educated, worshiped the risen Lord together in the joy of the Holy Spirit.

During the decade of the 1980s, lifestyle evangelism at Te Atatu resulted in about one thousand conversions! Some of the new converts were poor and jobless. So the congregation began developing a variety of ministries to assist both these new believers and other needy folk as well. A farm for drug rehabilitation, a modestly priced housing cooperative, emergency accommodation, a trust providing interest-free loans, and a Christian bookstore have all been a part of Te Atatu's community life. So are miraculous signs and wonders. In the power of the Spirit, bodies have been healed, drug addicts restored, broken marriages renewed, and non-Christians led to Christ.

I visited Te Atatu again in 1990, this time with my wife, Arbutus, and daughter, Sonya. Again we witnessed the presence of the kingdom. We stayed with one of the eldership team, Brian Hathaway, and his wife, Noeleen. We were impressed with the way their daughter, Sharon, quickly and easily included Sonya in her youth group's activities of worshiping, playing, and witnessing. It all started in late 1978. A small Plymouth Brethren congregation had been struggling hard for several years over whether all the gifts of the Spirit described in Acts were also for today. Finally they agreed that the answer was yes. The result was explosive church growth! The congregation grew from ninety adults and teenagers in 1978 to six hundred-fifty, ten years later.

There are now three sister congregations with a total of about one thousand people (including children). They seek to live out a powerfully articulated kingdom vision. They understand and seek to live the meaning of Christian community. And they integrate evangelism and social concern in the power of the Spirit. "Words, deeds, and signs" is their motto.

"We have a vision" is a ringing confession written by the church in 1986. Their vision is for a community of kingdom people:

"who recognize that the church is a new society;
who are available to each other, liable for each other, and accountable to each other;
who have voluntarily assumed a standard of living below (sometimes well below) what their income could allow;
who seek to correct the causes of poverty as well as release the poor from their immediate need."

"We have a vision of community," they declare, "whose lifestyle is so radically contradictory to the world's ways and thinking . . . that it may bring . . . immeasurable glory and praise to the Lord whom we love and serve."

Te Atatu's kingdom vision includes both the inward journey of community life within the body of believers and the outward journey of mission in the world.

Spirited worship, small groups, and economic sharing are central parts of their inner-body life. Their inexpensive cement-block church building probably does not attract people, but the quality of their worship and common life certainly do. Their singing, praying, and preaching come alive with a restrained but unmistakably charismatic spirit.

That's what Mandy Matthews experienced when she walked into a Sunday-evening service at Te Atatu in 1985. She knew very little about Christian faith, but an inner yearning had led her to visit one church after another. Nothing happened until she and a friend walked into the middle of a Te Atatu worship service. "When I opened the doors, we just got hit full blast with the Holy Spirit. Their faces were just shining. And I remember saying, 'Whatever this is, I want it.'"[1] That night, someone from Te Atatu explained the way of salvation to Mandy and she became a Christian—thanks initially to the power and beauty of Te Atatu's worship.

The small groups are where persons receive individual care and nurture. They encourage all new Christians to join a small group after they complete an introductory biblical series. More than half of the people in the three congregations are in these small groups that meet every week.

Economic sharing at Te Atatu begins at home—within the church family. The neighborhood around the church is multiracial. A few fairly wealthy sections are scattered through the largely lower-middle-class neighborhood. In the last few years, New Zealand's economy has been weak. Unemployment is high. Not surprisingly, major economic needs within the church have arisen, especially as they have led substantial numbers of poorer neighbors to Christ.

"Acts in Action" is their term for programs of economic sharing within the congregation, run by the deacons. When government funding for health care declined dramatically, poorer members literally had to choose between eating and going to the doctor. The church developed the Rapha Medical Fund so that the poorer members of the congregation could continue to receive adequate medical care. Wealthier members join the fund, even though they will never use it. Poorer members also contribute, even if only a dollar a week. Fifteen to twenty of the neediest members regularly draw from the fund for doctor's visits and prescriptions.

The Jireh Food Bank started out giving away free groceries. Rather quickly, however, they decided that any members who asked for free groceries more than twice should be offered help with their budgeting. Today, the deacons regularly counsel members on family budgets, make outright gifts where appropriate, help consolidate loans, and arrange for low- or no-interest loans through a church-related trust. As the budgeting assistance developed, they also decided it would be better for everyone if they sold the food—at a discount—at the food bank. Today, the church buys food at discount prices and sells it at cost. Needy members purchase their food at these low rates and then receive an additional refund of twenty percent at the church office. About fifteen families use the food bank regularly. Clear teaching about the church as community, plus generous sharing by members with more resources, makes possible these programs of economic caring within the fellowship.

Evangelism has always been a central concern at Te Atatu. Over the years, they have provided support for twenty-five missionaries in other countries. That their strong encouragement of missionary work is successful is demonstrated by the fact that eighteen of these missionaries are from Te Atatu itself.

Their evangelism, however, is not limited to people across the ocean. In the decade following the new beginning in late 1978, they were used by God to bring one thousand people to Christ. Most of these have come to faith through friendship evangelism and others through their many social ministries. In fact, none of their staff focus largely on evangelism, but they encourage everyone to share their faith. Their elders also teach that we can spread the Good News by word and deed.

One of the very simple but quite important things that Te Atatu has learned is that non-Christians are usually delighted to have someone pray for them at the end of some act of kindness or sharing. Brian Hathaway, teaching elder at Te Atatu for the last twenty-two years, explains that "it's amazing how many situations you'll find where people are very happy to be prayed for." So he encourages his people, whenever they help with some physical or material need, to ask at the end if the person would like to be prayed for. Almost always, they gladly agree. "It gives God an opportunity," Brian adds, "to draw attention to His work by answering, in dramatic ways sometimes."

Evangelism at Te Atatu is low-key. It is mostly friendship

evangelism. Many of the friendships begin with social contacts with non-Christians made possible by their many social ministries. "These community ministries," Brian explains, "enable Christians to rub shoulders with non-Christians, to minister to needs, to bring the love of Christ into people's lives." Frequently a gentle offer to pray for someone provides the transition from helping with a material concern to a conversation about spiritual need. Te Atatu's low-key friendship evangelism works! Over the last decade-plus, they have led about two people to Christ every week.

Brian does not think evangelism and social action ever conflict, but he confesses that "it's easier sometimes to meet physical need than it is to proclaim the Gospel in word. I suspect that it is probably easier to drift into a social-concern mode and to put evangelism on the back burner." He is very concerned about the way "many great social works that have been birthed out of evangelistic zeal have often finished up just empty shells of nothing more than philanthropy." Brian's solution is simple: "We're always encouraging [our] people to share their faith, whether at work, whether they are involved in social ministry, whether they are involved in a sports club, or across the fence with their neighbors."

In 1990, Brian published an important book, *Beyond Renewal: The Kingdom of God*[2] that shows how social ministry is a central part of what kingdom people do. His church practices what they preach. Large numbers of people at Te Atatu are engaged in a wide variety of social ministries.

Brian is very clear about the biblical foundations for these ministries. "We believe that God is committed to ministering to the poor, so we're committed to those in need. We believe Jesus spent a lot of his time ministering to those in need, the disadvantaged, the sick, the youth, the widows, the women. He was committed to those who were in some way abused or spurned by society."

Te Atatu's philosophy and structure for social ministry, however, is unusual. The church itself does not operate or control these ministries. Rather, church leaders sketch the broad vision, encourage members to dream dreams and organize projects, and then pastor the people as they carry out the programs. "As elders, we paint the big picture," Brian says. "And the big picture for us is that we are committed to evangelism and social concern in the power of the Holy Spirit." But the church leadership does not oversee the social ministries. Rather, they focus on nurturing and pastoring and supporting the people who do. "All the elders do," Brian insists, "is encourage them, support them, pastor them, communicate for them, profile for them what they are doing so the church is aware of how people are ministering to people."

That support includes prayer breakfasts, special banquets for everyone engaged in social ministries, special opportunities to call for volunteers—and above all, affirmation and pastoral counsel. "We believe," Brian adds, "that the principle of running a good church is not holding people, not controlling people. It's releasing people to run with what God is calling them to do."

Te Atatu has more than two dozen social ministries, but very few of them have any structural relationship with the church. They are independently controlled and financed. But it does make sense to consider them ministries of Te Atatu. Why? Because the pastoral leadership of the church invests a great deal of time and energy in nurturing and caring for the people who lead these ministries.

Not surprisingly, that kind of philosophy and pastoral support attracts Christians interested in social ministry to Te Atatu. That is why June Kelsall and her family began attending. Marvelously converted and delivered from addiction to tranquilizers and alcohol, June began to develop what is now Dayspring Trust—which operates several residential homes for abused women and single mothers unable to make it alone. The homes offer a safe living environment, training in budgeting and parenting, and counseling.

June had already begun to develop these programs before she joined Te Atatu. "But I wanted a pastor who personally had a heart for what I was doing," June says. "I went there because I saw a church with a heart for the community, and I saw the way they supported people in community work. And I wanted that kind of support." June gets encouragement, volunteers, and prayer support. On one occasion, Te Atatu also provided a no-interest loan for one of her residential homes.

The story of how June started what is now a large ministry at Dayspring Trust is an encouragement to all who care about the problems around them but feel overwhelmed when they think of starting anything big. Some years ago, June and a small interdenominational women's praise group she led began to sense a call to go into "the highways and byways." So they prayed for direction for six months. "Because we were very ordinary women," June says, "he gave us very simple directions." All they felt led to do was organize a drop-in center where people could drink tea and chat. "We all felt we were capable of making tea and smiling Jesus-smiles and caring for people." June is grateful that they did not have to start big: "If the Lord had given us great big instructions, we probably would have run the other way."

One day a lonely man dropped in at their "Care and Conversation" center. After a dramatic conversion, he brought in dozens and dozens of folk who needed love over the next few months. From that small beginning Dayspring has developed into a large program that includes three residential homes for poor (often abused) women and their children. Most of the hundreds of thousands of dollars of annual funding comes from secular sources, including government agencies. But all the staff and board members are Christians from a number of area churches. "The sort of care we give," June says, "is love with no strings attached. They don't have to come to the Lord, but they do!"

June tells the story of Rita to illustrate the impact of Dayspring Trust. Rita had lost her husband, and her ten grown children were gone. Depressed and mentally disturbed, she would not allow anyone even to touch her when she first came to June's program. But prayer has always been central to Dayspring Trust (the committee meets every week from 9:30–12:30 to pray for the work). So they prayed fervently, "Lord, show us how to touch her."

Soon they discovered that the little children at the home were climbing on her lap. Rita was great with children, so they gave her more and more children to care for. Soon Rita began to smile, then to volunteer her expert knitting skills to make clothing for the children. Before long, she was helping in almost everything.

One day, in a Bible study, Rita started to cry. "I really want to know this Jesus because I have known the love that has come through your whole-care center." Rita became a Christian, attended Te Atatu for awhile, and then returned to the Catholic church of her youth. A year ago, Rita died—but not before God had transformed her life and she, in turn, had brought love and joy to others.

Between the Banks Trust is one of Te Atatu's more important ministries. It started in 1980 as a vehicle to channel back into the community the profits from their successful store selling books, crafts, and gifts. Today the Trust uses these funds plus other substantial loans and gifts for three programs: short-term emergency financial help; longer-term loans; and assisting new or expanding ministries. Some of the help goes to people outside the church. If a person or family has a financial emergency, he or she can apply for a small no-interest loan, plus help with budgeting, from the Trust. When appropriate, the Trust also gives outright grants.

A number of Te Atatu ministries have started or received help from the Trust. One of Dayspring's residential houses became possible because of a major loan from the Trust. A large Christian outdoors ministry, Adventure Specialties, began initially under the umbrella of the Trust. An emergency-housing program still operates under the Trust's umbrella. The Family Care Center also has an ongoing relationship with the Trust.

The Family Care Center (FCC) provides a marvelous illustration of how Te Atatu's unique approach works out in practice. FCC is a private, Christian medical practice that works closely with the church to offer medical care that is concerned about the whole person.

The story starts with Dr. X. (There seems to be a special modesty connected with everyone at Te Atatu. He adamantly insisted that I not use his name!) Nine years ago, this good Christian doctor became increasingly unhappy in his work because the medical practice he shared with two other doctors did not give him the freedom he wanted to share his faith and pray with patients. He knew about the wholistic ministry of the Te Atatu Bible Chapel. He also knew that the neighborhood around the church lacked adequate medical service, so he joined the church and set up his own medical practice in the neighborhood.

Dr. X was not interested in a second-rate medical practice

serving as an excuse for evangelism. "First and foremost," he insists, "the service has to be a professional medical service, not some Christian people wanting to evangelize and tacking on a medical service." But he also knew that forty percent to fifty percent of the folk who came to his office came because of problems that were not really medical—they had social problems and spiritual needs. So he made sure that all his staff were committed Christians who shared his vision of "lifestyle evangelism—building up friendships and relationships." At the right time, when they sense an openness to spiritual needs, they talk about them and offer to pray with people.

Links to the chapel offer many resources. Dr. X and one of the nurses are members of the fellowship. When people need emergency food, clothing, housing, or baby-sitting, Dr. X can arrange it through the chapel. Women at the church prepare frozen meals that he can offer to a sick mom unable to cook. Pastor Gordon Stewart from the chapel comes over every Monday for lunch to pray with Dr. X and the staff about patients with special needs. Some of the patients are poorer church members whose bills are covered through the church's Rapha Medical Fund (usually he does not bother to bill the church!). And Dr. X chose to rent office space from the church's Trust so that rental income could be cycled back into the community.

Recently, one of Dr. X's patients was devastated when she lost her baby halfway through her pregnancy. This woman was in her third marriage. Trauma had stalked her life. When she became pregnant again, FCC not only provided its normal, thorough, loving care but they also committed themselves to praying regularly for her. Soon after a lovely baby arrived, the grandmother sent them a grateful thank-you for their good care. "What the [grand]mother didn't acknowledge," Dr. X adds, "was that God's hand was there in that as well." But he is not impatient. "At some point in the future I look forward to an opportunity when I can say to her, when she talks about her granddaughter, how I see that as God's answer to much praying."

Christian Surfers is another ministry related to Te Atatu. Mark and Tina started Christian Surfers as a low-key way to share the Gospel. Their evangelistic strategy has two stages: "One is serving and winning people's respect, and [the other is] then presenting the Gospel when their ears are open." Kids surf during the day and listen to testimonies in the evening. It is much easier for a Christian to invite non-Christian friends to Christian Surfers than to ask them to come to church.

Mark and Tina started Christian Surfers in 1984 (since then, it has spread to several other countries) while attending another church. But increasingly they felt unsupported in their unusual ministry. In fact, the church kept pestering them to do youth groups and other activities inside the church. Therefore, about four years ago, they moved to Te Atatu because they needed pastoral support for what God had called them to do beyond the walls of the local church. "There's been instant recognition," they gratefully report, "that we're ministering outside the church."

Adventure Specialties runs a vast variety of outdoor camping, hiking, and kayaking expeditions. The founders, Lyndsay and Glenda, were members at Te Atatu as their vision developed in the early '80s. Brian and others at the chapel offered strong encouragement and financial support. In fact, they started under the umbrella of Between the Banks Trust, but they soon became an independent organization. By 1991, they were serving about twelve hundred people a year.

The evangelistic component of Adventures Specialties is very low-key. Seldom are there organized times for worship and prayer, but the instructors often are able to develop close personal relationships that have an impact on people's lives.

James[3] went on one of their trips run for the Salvation Army's Kickstart Program. High unemployment is devastating many New Zealand families. The Kickstart Program serves unemployed dads and their families.

One Monday morning, after nine years of work, James's company laid him off. In his mid-forties with a modest education, James applied for over fifty jobs—and missed them all. His self-esteem plummeted, and his family was in trouble.

In his first week-long trip with Adventure Specialties, James poured out his heart. He shared the struggles in his family and the bad relationship with his teenage son. So they arranged for James and his son to go together on a week-long trip, camping and kayaking on gorgeous Great Barrier Island. On that trip, the father-son relationship was wonderfully restored. James is not yet a Christian, but he is becoming more involved with the church programs at the Salvation Army. Adventure Specialties did not produce instant transformation in James's life, but they contributed to a process that may, in God's time, change his life.

Bikers for Christ (BFC) is more overtly evangelistic. Two chapel members—Grant Chayter and Mike Bregman—started BFC about six years ago. Four of the five active members are from Te Atatu. They just hang out on Darby Street, where the motorcycle folk congregate and make friends. If the right opportunity arises, they switch from discussing bikes to discussing Jesus. Martin is one of the bikers who came to Christ. Now he is part of the team. "We all were motorcyclists before we became Christians," Martin says. "It's easier for us to talk bikes and then talk Christ than it is for an evangelist to come and talk Christ."

Te Atatu has many other ministries. Massey Caregivers includes about twenty people who offer almost any practical help people request—transportation to the hospital, baby-sitting, or help with washing the floors. A Clothing Exchange supplies five-to-ten families a week with needed used clothing. Care Share Ministries operates a home for boys. The Japanese Exchange Program assists Japanese youth who come to New Zealand to study. The Vegetable Co-op provides modestly priced vegetables for the community. Where Te Atatu's members see a need, they try to meet it in the name of Christ.

Not everything works. And programs keep changing. The People Helping People Trust built fifty-four modestly priced homes in the mid-1980s before it folded. A job-training program assisted a couple hundred people in the early to mid-'80s and then stopped. Te Atatu's decentralized approach means that programs last only as long as the vision, enthusiasm, and fund-raising ability of the organizers. Sometimes duplication occurs, or people get lost between loosely coordinated programs.

The failure of the 4221 Trust illustrates the weak side of Te Atatu's decentralized organizational structure. The 4221's goal was to rehabilitate street kids. At its height, it included a farm for drug rehabilitation and a T-shirt store to finance the ministry. It started with help from Between the Banks Trust, but the leadership moved away from the church and eventually 4221 collapsed.

Steve and Jo-Anne Woodward recently started one of the newest ministries—soon after they made a strong commitment to Christ at Te Atatu. Steve is a native New Zealander (Maori). Jo-Anne is European.

Four years ago, both Steve and Jo-Anne were, at best, very lukewarm Christians. Sometimes they made it to church; sometimes they didn't.

Fortunately, Steve met Brian Hathaway one day in 1988, and Brian invited Steve to the chapel. Desperate, Steve started attending regularly and renewed his commitment. After working for eleven and a half years as a security guard, he had just lost his job. Debts were piling up fast. Steve found support of many kinds in the small group he joined at Te Atatu. The small group donated money to cover some of the debts. When Brian learned of a large credit-card debt, he arranged a no-interest loan through Between the Banks Trust.

Jo-Anne did not join Steve immediately in his new journey of faith. When she did, she quickly slipped back. Then a few months later, she recommitted her life to Christ. Since then, their faith has grown steadily.

Steve is still unemployed, so they would be without adequate health care but for Te Atatu's Rapha Medical Fund. For five dollars a month, they get good care, and they buy their food at inexpensive prices at the church's food co-op. "We don't have to make the decision," Steve says, "whether we are going to take the kids to the doctor or put the meal on the table. There's money here for both."

Grateful for the church's help, they decided to do something for others. In 1992, they formed Helping Hands, which already assists about thirty unemployed families, single parents, and other low-income folk.

That's the story of Te Atatu. It's a story about a loving church community that brings people to strong faith in Christ and then ministers to all their needs. Empowered, they in turn reach out to strengthen others.

Sometimes people stumble as they try to help others. Good

intentions do not guarantee good results. Te Atatu's decentralized structure has advantages and disadvantages.

Modest as usual, Brian Hathaway is the first to acknowledge that Te Atatu is still on pilgrimage. "We've got plenty of weaknesses. No church has it all together. I guess we are a few steps down the pathway of integration of the work of the Spirit with social concern and evangelism. But that's all we are, just a few steps down the path."

If twenty percent of the local churches in the world today were half as far along the path as Te Atatu Bible Chapel, Christians would turn the world upside down.

1   Except where otherwise indicated, quotations in this chapter come from personal interviews.

2   Brian Hathaway, *Beyond Renewal: The Kingdom of God* (Word, [U.K.], 1990). See also Hathaway's article, "The Spirit and Social Action—A Model," *Transformation*, October-December 1988, 40–43. Hathaway was a key organizer of the group of New Zealand leaders who drafted the Kingdom Manifesto—see *Transformation*, July-September 1990, 6–11.

3   The name has been changed.

6
Stomach Theology in a Poor Island Paradise

I would go around and when I saw somebody who needed help, I just helped them. There are not very many people who have compassion.

Wayan Mastra

How would you share Christ on an island paradise where family, land, and Hindu faith are so tightly entwined that conversion means loss of property, friends, family, even a decent burial?

The gorgeous little island of Bali has often been described as a lost paradise.[1] Today over a million tourists visit this small Indonesian island located just east of Java. It is only one hundred miles long and fifty miles wide, but it has breathtaking beaches and soaring mountains. For centuries, however, the rough seas and coral reefs around its rugged coastline kept out many would-be foreign conquerors. As most of what is now Indonesia became Muslim over the course of the fifteenth and sixteenth centuries, Bali remained Hindu. Even the Dutch, who controlled most of Indonesia by 1750, did not conquer Bali until 1914.

Bali Hinduism is a unique mixture of ancient animism, ancestor worship, magic, and Hinduism. Through a complex system of rules and religious ritual, the Balinese seek to maintain a harmony between the high Hindu gods who dwell in the volcanic mountains at the center of the island and the evil powers of the underworld. Every village has its own temples, and every family has its own shrine. Personal identity is so intertwined with the land, ancestors, and rituals of the village that any change of religion produces enormous inner confusion and powerful community hostility.

The Dutch colonial government banned Christian missionaries—both to avoid trouble and also to preserve Bali's unique Hindu culture that Western scholars "discovered" in the 1920s. But in 1929, a Chinese evangelist, Tsang To Han, won permission to minister to a few Christian Chinese immigrants. Soon he and another itinerant missionary were preaching to the native Balinese. Hundreds responded and received baptism.

Tsang harshly condemned Balinese Hinduism as demonic superstition and urged the new converts to break sharply with Bali culture. The result was intensive persecution. Angry neighbors cut off converts' irrigation water, destroyed their crops, burned down their houses, and denied them burial places in the village. Furious, they rejected the new Christians as "culture despisers" and "black Dutch."

Fearing further chaos, the Dutch authorities offered the Christians some land in a malaria-infested swamp full of insects, snakes, and tigers. To the relief of everyone else, many of the new Christian families moved in 1939 to this hostile jungle thought to be the abode of evil spirits. The Christians named it *Blimbingsari* after a delicious star fruit that flourished there.

The Hindus all expected this little band of Christian renegades who had broken the harmony of Balinese life and angered the ancestral spirits to die and disappear. Instead, they prospered. They carved a village out of the jungle in the shape of a cross, planted crops, and built homes. Over the next decades, especially after the economic development programs in the late '70s, Blimbingsari became widely known throughout Bali as one of the cleanest, healthiest, and most prosperous villages on the island.

Slowly the Gospel continued to spread. Not all Christians had moved to Blimbingsari, although that became the center of the Christian Protestant Church in Bali. In the early 1960s, frequent instances of miraculous healing convinced many to become Christians. By 1965, the church had grown to six thousand five hundred.

The year 1965 was a fateful one, both for a young Balinese named Wayan Mastra and also for the whole country of Indonesia. Wayan was born into a typical Hindu family in East Bali, but his father, who had taught himself to read and write, gladly encouraged his young son's love of learning. Most villagers left school to work in the fields after grade three. For Wayan the nearest primary school was more than six miles away, but he determined to study, so he walked six miles every morning and evening for six years. After secondary school in a distant town, he attended a Christian college in Java, where he accepted Christ.

For a year he struggled over whether to tell his father. Wayan still had vivid memories of the time during his childhood when a Christian died and the Hindu community refused to allow burial in the village. It had taken four truckloads of police to escort the body to another burial ground. Finally, he took the plunge, told his parents, and moved to Jakarta to study theology.

Mastra's first few years of pastoral work were stunningly successful. When he started, in 1960, his congregation had one other member—his wife Ketut! But Mastra combined vigorous preaching with care for the whole person. "I would just go around," Mastra remembers, "and when I saw somebody who needed help, I just helped them. There are not very many people who have compassion."[2] When the Gunung Hgang volcano erupted in March 1963, killing thousands and driving more from their homes, Mastra offered help to everyone in need. The response was overwhelming. Within a little more than four years, he had baptized three hundred-fifty people and started five congregations.

In 1965, however, anyone working with the poor in Bali was in great danger. Communism was growing rapidly in Indonesia. An unsuccessful Communist coup triggered the slaughter of huge numbers of Communists all across Indonesia. Anyone who seemed concerned for the poor, even devout Christians like Mastra, were suspect. So he accepted an invitation to do doctoral work in the U.S.A. and left Bali just two weeks before a massive purge of all suspected Communists swept through Bali. Had he been there, he almost certainly would have died.

When Dr. Mastra returned in 1971, both he and the church were ready for change. At that point, virtually every aspect of church life—music, architecture, worship—was Western. Balinese Christians, however, were sick of the label "black Dutch." They wanted to end their isolation from Bali culture.

Mastra likes to say that Bali is his body, but Christ is his life. He chaired the watershed synod of 1972, held at Abianbase, where the church adopted a new policy for Christian mission in Bali. First they decided to build a cultural and training center called *Dhyana Pura* (Temple of Meditation), which would use Balinese architecture and art. Their goal was to proclaim the Gospel in ways relevant to the Balinese people, "to help Balinese Christians to gain a greater appreciation of their cultural heritage within the context of their faith and to find new ways of expressing that faith within the culture."[3]

Mastra found a willing ally for the adaptation of Balinese art forms in Nyoman Darsane, now a world-renowned Bali artist. Darsane had grown up in a Hindu home and become a Christian while studying in Java. Darsane loves to use his art to share the Gospel. He has written fifty new hymns, using a Balinese style, and teaches music in the churches. He uses traditional shadow puppets to tell Bible stories. He has written a drama with traditional song and dance. And his paintings—which are now in great demand around the world—frequently deal with biblical themes.

Economic development was also high on the agenda of the 1972 synod. They resolved to help villagers learn new skills in farming, nutrition, health, and family planning. Realizing the economic importance of the mushrooming tourist industry, they determined to learn how to enable the people of Bali to gain greater social and financial benefits from the tourists. Cooperatives, counseling, and vocational and cultural training for the youth were all on the agenda. So was greater interreligious dialogue with their Hindu neighbors.

Mastra's goal in the 1972 synod was "a balanced Church ministry—a wholistic ministry where we both concentrate on building up the church itself in self-sufficiency, and also in becoming a community which will be a blessing to others."[4] The idea of blessing is central to Mastra's vision. He thinks the Bali church should grow in the same four ways Jesus did according to Luke 2:52: in wisdom, stature, favor with God, and favor with the people. A church that grows academically, culturally, spiritually, and socially can be a blessing to its neighbors in all four areas.

Mastra's concern is to enter a person's life and person "through three doors: the head, the heart, and the stomach. It is like the Lord's Prayer: (1) Give us this day our daily bread—that is for the stomach; (2) forgive us our trespasses—that is for the mind or the head; (3) lead us not into temptation—that is for the heart."

Mastra is by no means concerned only with economic growth. He strongly supports the church's major investment in education. His agenda of developing culturally indigenous forms of worship and architecture promotes cultural growth that brings new social acceptance with Hindu neighbors. And he is deeply committed to spiritual growth through both evangelism and spiritual nurture within the church.

Mastra, however, does not hesitate for a second to advocate economic growth. He thinks the strong persecution and resulting poverty that the early Bali Christians faced led to a misguided theology of suffering. (He also suspects the Dutch colonialists emphasized poverty to keep the Balinese weak so they could "rule us forever.") Mastra wants to replace that attitude with a "stomach theology" that builds a self-sufficient church with adequate resources to care for itself and share with others.[5] Christians are not supposed to be poor. "To be a Christian," Mastra says, "you must be a capitalist." Quickly he explains that comment with Jesus' parable of the talents. All should use their talents to multiply their capital. God "always encourages you to make money."

The next key question for Mastra is what Christians do with their new resources. They should not use them largely for consumer goods for themselves. Instead, he wants his newly well-off Balinese Christians to give generously to the church and the poor. "We must get money to help the poor," he insists, "but we must not be poor, see? The whole theology must be changed. That's why in Bali we first change the people's mental attitudes, change the theology. Secondly, we have to provide some skills. And thirdly, we have to give them capital. That's why in Bali we have the Dhyana Pura lay-training center (which includes biblical training). We have the school, Widya Pura, a school to train the brain. And we have credit unions (MBM), to enable people to get some capital. And when we build these people, they will be a blessing to (other) people."

Economic growth, however, does not happen merely because

theologians call for it. Four years after the 1972 synod's ringing call for change, the Bali church was still very poor—so poor, in fact, that they could not afford to pay the pastors. The devastating earthquake in 1976 made things even worse. It even destroyed a new church building at the Bali church's home base, Blimbingsari.

Fortunately, an Australian businessman and builder, David Bussau, agreed to come and help. David, Carol, and their two daughters moved to Blimbingsari in late 1976 to help rebuild the church. The nearest water supply, needed to mix the concrete, was about three miles away, so the church building waited for a year while David helped build a dam and a water line. Interestingly, the best route for the water went through a Hindu village. Thus, Hindus got water first, but eventually the water supply reached the Christian village of Blimbingsari. They built a lovely church implementing Mastra's vision of using Balinese architecture and art in the Christian community. Today over one thousand Christians worship there.

The water supply from the new dam also transformed the area's agriculture. Christians and Hindus doubled their rice crops. Meanwhile David Bussau sparked a whole series of projects in community development. First a health clinic in Blimbingsari that also served surrounding Hindu villages, then new roads, English lessons taught by Carol, and a children's playground. Blimbingsari won award after award for its record rice crops and the quality of its village life.

In 1980, David Bussau's and Wayan Mastra's partnership in economic development entered a new, even more significant phase . The Bussaus had returned to Australia in 1979, but Mastra invited them back to Bali in 1980 to help with the church's new training center, Dhyana Pura, to help make it a profitable conference center and also set up a training program for Christian and Hindu youth that would prepare them to work in the tourist industry.

Dhyana Pura is another striking result of the important synod of 1972. The church was able to acquire a gorgeous beach-front property at Seminyak, Kuta Beach. Mastra made sure that the buildings and tropical gardens they built were pure Balinese. Dedicated in 1977, Dhyana Pura was to be a cultural and training center for the church—a place for spiritual enrichment, including biblical training for pastors and laity. It was also to be a job-training center and a hotel for tourists. Today, Dhyana Pura is an internationally famous conference center with eighty-six rooms, a restaurant, and a swimming pool. More than two thousand students have graduated from its training programs in tourism.

Dr. Ketut Waspada, bishop of the church from 1988–92, now oversees the hotel training program at Dhyana Pura. This program is designed not only to create jobs but also to avoid some of the terrible evils of the tourist industry. The lovely little island of Bali is the center of tourism for all of Indonesia. Over a million come every year. So do prostitution, disease, and corruption. Dr. Waspada and others realized that their young people were running after money and forgetting what it means to be human.

A visit to the tourist belt of the Philippines in 1986 frightened Waspada. As he saw the ghastly, widespread prostitution including large numbers of young girls ages twelve to fourteen, he feared for what could happen "in my country on my lovely island of Bali—especially if my own daughter would also do like that."

Waspada helped start some additional training programs in 1987. Devotions and Christian ethics are an important part of the curriculum. They want to help the students learn how to serve tourists without losing their human dignity. The one-year program trains youth for front office and room service. The two year program trains supervisors. Seventy-five to eighty percent of the graduates quickly find work—partly because many of the personnel managers were former students.

Only two to three percent of the students in these programs are Christians, so they try to weave an introduction to Christian faith into the courses. But thus far, according to Waspada, only one person has become a Christian through this program.

As it turned out, the training programs at Dhyana Pura begun by David Bussau in 1980 were only the beginning of a very creative partnership between Bussau and Dr. Mastra. Everywhere Dr. Mastra saw new economic needs and opportunities. Just as regularly, Bussau was able to implement programs and locate resources. New schools, roads, health clinics, and safe drinking water all followed.

Rather quickly they realized that a revolving-credit plan could become a central key, so they developed a program to make small loans at market rates to individuals and groups who could thereby develop successful, small businesses that created new jobs and income. Rapidly the program spread across Bali and gave birth to a whole new organization in the Bali church called the Maha Bhoga Marga (MBM).

Today MBM is a large organization that has improved living standards for tens of thousands of people in Bali. The 1993 budget for MBM and the bank it operates was about two and a half million U.S. dollars. More than twenty of its more than fifty full-time staff have university training. In addition, MBM has spun off similar, rapidly growing, daughter organizations in other parts of Indonesia.

The name of this community development organization has a wonderful meaning: "The most excellent way to both physical and spiritual food, based on a right relationship with God and others."[6] Priyadi Reksasiswaya, who served as director for the first twelve years, states the purpose in simple terms: "As Christians, we would like to show the love of Christ to the people." And in fact eighty-five to ninety percent of MBM's programs are with Hindus.

When the church synod launched MBM in 1982, they spelled out very clearly the theological foundations of their ambitious new program of economic development. These included: (1) "a belief in the dignity and high potential of all people created in the image of God;" (2) "a belief in God's mission of PEACE—between people and Himself, people and people, people and the earth's resources—through Jesus Christ the Lord;" (3) "a belief that models of God's kingdom play a prophetic role in relationship to government."[7]

MBM is "stomach theology" at work. Its major programs are: small loans through a system of revolving credit; a Rice Bank; an experimental farm; and vocational training.

Out in the villages, people could not get tiny loans of fifty dollars or two hundred dollars to purchase a few pigs, buy eggs to market, purchase a sewing machine, or start growing orchids for sale. They had no capital to serve as collateral. Anyway, it was not worth a bank's time to make such tiny loans. Within a few years, however, MBM discovered that precisely these small loans created jobs and wealth in an amazing way.

Pak Tegeg is a Hindu who got his first loan—for fifty-four dollars!—from MBM in 1983. A local Christian liked his pottery and wanted to place a modest order, but Pak Tegeg did not have the financial ability to expand production enough to handle the request. Fortunately, the Christian friend told him about MBM"s small-loan program. Pak Tegeg has since repaid that first loan plus five more. His business has grown sevenfold, and his pottery business provides the income for twenty-four families. In fact, he has grown to a point where regular banks are glad to loan him money. Pak Tegeg is still a Hindu, but he respects Christians in a new way.

From 1983–1991, MBM made 8,998 loans that created 22,638 new jobs. Over ninety-nine percent of the loans were repaid with interest. Initially, the capital came through Western donors, especially a U.S. partner, now called Opportunity International. But since this is a revolving-credit program, repayments return to MBM, which simply reloans the money as soon as it is repaid. Year after year, the initial Western capital keeps creating new jobs. And the reasonable interest that MBM charges covers its overhead costs.

Pastors are a key link in the loan program. When a person asks for a loan, the first step is an interview with the local Christian pastor—whether the person asking for a loan is a Hindu or a Christian. In fact, over eighty-five percent of the loans have gone to Hindus! MBM runs seminars to train the pastors for this key role. If the pastor recommends the person, then MBM evaluates the business plan to see if it will work. Sometimes they suggest a more workable approach. Every proposed loan must be likely to create at least one new job. And if a Christian, the loan recipient must agree to tithe ten percent of the profit to the church; or, if a Hindu, give ten percent to community programs. Once the loan is approved, the local pastor again monitors repayment made in tiny amounts over a number of months. Less than one percent fails to repay the loan. MBM also runs seminars on management that incorporate Christian principles of stewardship and prosperity.

MBM's Rice Bank helps very poor farmers escape the tyranny of loan sharks. Without any storage facilities, poor farmers had to sell their rice crop at harvest time at very low prices. Then a few months later they needed to purchase rice for food and seed at much higher prices! Often that meant a loan from a loan shark at interest as high as seventy percent after a few months.

The Rice Bank organizes poor farmers into tiny cooperatives of five families each. Each co-op receives an initial loan at modest interest rates so that the members can purchase rice for food and planting. At harvest they can sell their rice and repay the loan, or store some rice at the Rice Bank until prices go up or they need it themselves. Rice stored at the Rice Bank by co-ops or individuals goes into a "Joseph Sack" that provides a constant reminder of the biblical story. And like the Israelites, many poor farmers in Bali and other parts of Indonesia are now escaping slavery because of Rice Banks like the one pioneered by MBM.

MBM also operates an experimental farm and vocational training programs. The farm has chickens, pigs, and a biotechnology laboratory. Loan recipients who are farmers sometimes come here for seminars. Training programs in furniture making, mechanics (including welding), and baking offer not only technical knowledge but also training in how to set up and manage a small business. In many different ways, MBM is contributing dramatically to improved living standards in Bali.

What has been the impact of these successful development programs on the church? Much is positive. Christians are no longer the poor class in Bali. Because of the economic development, the church is much closer to economic self-sufficiency. In fact, in 1975, there were only nineteen pastors, and ninety percent of their support came from the West. By 1991, there were forty-eight pastors, and eighty-five percent of their support came from their local congregation! Their emphasis on economic growth and tithing is working.

Increasingly, too, the Hindu community accepts the church. Christians, after all, have brought them not only thousands of loans but also roads, bridges, mobile clinics, training programs, and educational opportunity. In former times, people turned automatically to the Hindu temple when they had problems. Increasingly, today they go to the Christian pastor when their cow is sick, or they cannot afford to send a child to school. Acceptance, gratitude, and respect are replacing anger and persecution. Much has improved.

There are also problems. There are vigorous internal debates. Nor have the development programs of MBM, thus far, resulted in rapid church growth within Bali.

Some feel that Bishop Mastra emphasizes material blessing too much. They fear that in the experimental farm and the total work of MBM, he overemphasizes making a profit rather than loving one's neighbor in Christ's name. They reject the notion that Christians can be a blessing to others only if they have material wealth. And they object to Mastra's statement that "to become a Christian you must be a capitalist."

What has been the evangelistic impact of the 1972 synod's vision and programs of culturally sensitive wholistic mission? It is not easy to answer that question. The Bali church today is not much larger than it was in 1965! Before we conclude that they have failed in the area of evangelism, however, we must explore their theology of mission, long-term strategy, and the large church growth they have nurtured in other Indonesian Islands.

Wayan Mastra has thought deeply over several decades about how to share Christ in Hindu Bali. Giving the Gospel "Balinese clothes" is essential. So is understanding that Bali Hinduism is a visual faith. Therefore words alone are not enough. Actions must dramatize and demonstrate verbal proclamation. "That is why the Bali church is active in social action, in improving the people's condition by building schools, dormitories, a hospital, an experimental farm, a chicken farm, and a fishpond as a demonstration of our love as well as a model for improving the people's condition."[8] One of the church's guidelines on witnessing insists that "an ounce of action is worth a ton of words."[9] That, Mastra says, is the "Eastern way of doing mission."

Another church guideline on witnessing underlines their concern not to attack the faith of their Hindu neighbors: Christian witness should not disrupt the community but, rather, transform it.[10] Mastra looks for the places in traditional Bali Hinduism that provide openings for Christian faith. Traditional Balinese, Mastra says, struggle less over sin and guilt than over anxiety and fear about the evil spirits, the oppression of the powerful, or the enormous cost of religious ritual, especially cremation.[11] So Mastra shows how Christian faith answers their deeply felt needs. In the process, the Gospel slowly transforms the whole culture.

Witra's story is a good example. When he lost his job, Witra decided to use black magic against his boss. But when he visited the person who formerly practiced black magic, he discovered that the man had become a Christian. The man referred him to his new pastor. So Witra asked the church pastor to use black magic against his boss! Instead, the pastor offered love and help in getting a new job. He also helped him move to another area with less crime and prostitution. Witra also was impressed that Christians had no fear of the evil spirits (in his village people were so afraid that they did not stay out after 9:00 P.M.). After a year of patient dialogue, Witra and his family were baptized. Two of Witra's brothers and a sister are now interested in Christianity. The pastor is also helping Witra talk about Christ to his parents and grandparents, who are impressed with his improved standard of living and the way he cares for them.

In the 1984 synod, the church developed a sixteen-year plan for the church. 1984–88 were to be the years of lay training and fellowship. 1988–92 focused on mission. 1992–96 would be devoted to service. And 1996–2000, they hope, will be the period of harvest.

In the first period of fellowship, they formed Penta Koinonia groups in each congregation. Each group has five families who meet in homes every other week for fellowship, prayer, and Bible study.

In the period of mission (1988–92), the church reemphasized the fact that all Christians have a responsibility for mission. It is not enough to talk about dramatic healing and frequent conversions in the 1960s. They must happen now. Mission is not first of all about sending missionaries somewhere else, but about each member's being ready to share Christ with his or her neighbors. In one special service in 1988, nine hundred people renewed their commitment to witness to Christ. The church has opened up forty-five new mission posts—places where Bible study and discussion take place with non-Christians who have expressed an interest in Christ. The ninety-six people from non-Christian families who came to Christ in 1991 seemed to be a confirmation of this renewed emphasis on mission.

Wayan Dibia began a new mission post soon after he was healed around Easter 1991. He had been lame and could not see well. But after Christians prayed for him, he was healed. Gladly, he became a Christian. Full of joy, he traveled to a nearby Hindu village to share his new faith, but he couldn't explain it very well so he invited people to visit his pastor. Fifteen families have now become Christians in that village. Fortunately the village leader, even though he and the village are Hindu, does not object, because his son is in a Christian school and he respects Christians.

From 1992 to 1996 is the period of service. During this period they are strengthening their long tradition of serving the needs of their Hindu neighbors. And 1996–2000 is to be the harvest period.

The Bali church has obviously adopted a long-term evangelistic design. In their hostile culture with tightly knit Hindu villages, it is very difficult for Hindus to accept Christ. They have decided to show that Christianity has Balinese clothes, that Christians care about their neighbors, and that Christian faith brings a better life. Over the long haul, they believe large numbers will come to Christ.

Christian schools have been one central part of this evangelistic plan since 1955. Recognizing that many parents were too poor to pay the fees for their children's education, the church began schools from kindergarten to high school and opened them to Hindus, Muslims, and Christians. The Bali name is *Widhya Pura*—house of knowledge. Today they have about twenty-five hundred students in different schools. Seventy percent of the students are Hindus, twenty-five percent Christians and five percent Muslims. They also operate five hostels (or dormitories) connected to the schools where four hundred-fifty students live. Sixty percent of the youth who live in the hostels are non-Christians when they come. Thirty percent of those become Christians while there. Christian worship and Bible study are a regular part of life in the schools and hostels.

Ketut Sudiana's father, a Hindu priest, could not afford to pay for his son's education, so a local Christian pastor said he could study at no cost at one of the church's schools. In 1976, Ketut moved to the hostel in Blimbingsari. A brilliant student, Ketut won top grades in the courses on Christianity. Teachers assumed he was a Christian and occasionally asked him to lead devotions. But he was still a Hindu.

After high school, however, he began to compare Hinduism and Christianity and eventually accepted Christ. When he told his parents that he wanted to be baptized, they resisted. Ketut persisted. Finally his parents said he must break totally with his community so they would not be ostracized. He left to study for the ministry. After a time, because of increased community pressure, his parents stopped answering his letters. Fortunately, the story did not end there. After seminary, he returned home and was able to reestablish a good relationship with his mother and father. They are still Hindus, but they respect their Christian son and attended his wedding. Ketut is now a pastor.

Ketut Sudiana's story shows how costly it is for Hindus in Bali to become Christians. Hindus now respect Christians far more than they did in 1939 or even 1972. They appreciate the educational opportunities and economic improvements that Christians have shared with the Hindu majority. Increasingly, Hindus turn to Christian pastors rather their Hindu priest when they need help. But accepting Christ is still extremely difficult for the Hindu villager who wants to remain in his or her own village. In fact in 1987–88, a Balinese law formalized traditional practice and declared that if a Hindu converted to Christianity, the person would lose all land, inheritance rights, and even the right to live or be buried in the village. Often they must move away if they want to accept Christ.

Perhaps that is why there are now almost three times as many Balinese Christians on several other Indonesian islands (especially Sulawesi) as there are in Bali itself. This story of transmigration is part of the Bali church's story of evangelism.

Bali's population explosion fuels the migration to Sulawesi. The tiny island of Bali is one of the more densely populated places on earth. Sulawesi, by contrast, had relatively few people in 1950.

So for several decades, the Indonesian government encouraged Balinese to migrate, offering every family five acres of land.

Most Balinese Hindus, however, found migration extremely difficult. Their gods lived at the center of the universe on the high mountains of Bali. Their ancestors' spirits dwelt in their home village. For Christians, who believe their God is everywhere, migration was much easier.

Persecution also encouraged Christians to migrate. When Imade Sureiandhade and his parents became Christians in the 1960s, the community cut off the water supply for their rice fields. Local shop owners refused to do business with them. This family chose to stay, but many other new converts preferred to start a new life in a less hostile setting. So from 1955 on, more and more Christians moved to Sulawesi.

The home church in Bali was supportive. They sent pastors. They provided some orientation though MBM for migrants. Eventually they helped the new church in Sulawesi establish its own community development organization modeled on MBM.

Migration to Sulawesi has proved to be an attractive option for a number of Bali Hindus. The life and witness of Balinese Christians has slowly convinced many that Christianity is preferable to Hinduism. But changing religions is very costly if they remain in their home villages. So they move to Sulawesi. "Over there they become Christians," Wayan Mastra says. "Here they are still Hindus because they are afraid, because many times to become Christian in Bali is a matter of life and death."

Letters or visits spread the word in Hindu Bali villages about the cheap land and growing prosperity in Sulawesi. When they move, the growing Balinese church in Sulawesi welcomes them. That's why today there are about twice as many Balinese Christians in Sulawesi as in Bali.

The same thing has happened as Bali Hindus have moved to other islands and the cities of Indonesia. The result is that today at least two-thirds and some estimates say as many as three-quarters of all Bali Christians live elsewhere.

When one reflects on the fact that the church in Bali itself is still about the same size as it was in 1965, one dare not quickly conclude that its evangelistic efforts have failed. Tripling or quadrupling in thirty years represents stunning success! And according to their own patient, long-range plan, harvest time is still to come—in 1996–2000.

It is too early to provide a final evaluation of the Bali church's wholistic model. It is possible that they have been too cautious in their direct evangelism in recent decades. It's possible that a fuller integration of the prayer for miraculous healings of the 1960s, more explicit witnessing, and the economic development of the 1970s and 1980s would have been even more fruitful. But only those who have grown more than three hundred percent or four hundred percent in the last thirty years dare cast stones. The Christian Protestant Church in Bali offers a powerful example of how to live the whole Gospel in a way that both respects and transforms local culture.

---

1 The material for this chapter comes from Douglas G. McKenzie with I. Wayan Mastra, *The Mango Tree Church: The Story of the Protestant Christian Church in Bali* (Brisbane: Boolarong Publications, 1988); I. Wayan Mastra, "A Contextualized Church: The Bali Experience," *Gospel in Context*, April 1978, 4–32; Christopher Sugden, *A Critical and Comparative Study of Wayan Mastra and Vinay Samuel* (Unpublished dissertation, Westminster College, Oxford, 1987); extensive personal interviews in Bali; and documents from the church and Maranatha Trust.

2 Unless otherwise indicated, quotations are from personal interviews.

3 Quoted in *Mango Tree Church*, 31.

4 Ibid., 33.

5 Ibid., 34.

6 Ibid., 60.

7 Ibid., 58.

8 Mastra, "A Contextualized Church," 20.

9 *Mango Tree Church* 72.

10 Ibid.

11 Mastra, "A Contextualized Church," 14.

7

Orphan, Businessman, and Banker for the Poor

Something of a cross between John Wesley and Adam Smith.

Far Eastern Economic Review

I want to tell you about a friend who takes a small gift of five hundred dollars and, in ten years, creates ten new jobs for the poorest in the world. Those ten jobs dramatically improve the lives of fifty family members and also help spread the Gospel. Meet David Bussau, one of my favorite businessmen. David helps make that happen in twenty-two different countries around the world today through the Opportunity Network he helped create.

These small loans make a difference in the lives of desperate people like Riasa, who lives in Indonesia. Riasa is a disabled widow with two dependents living in a society with no disability pension, no health benefits and no unemployment benefits. Her small house with a thatched roof has no electricity, no running water, no toilet—just a mud floor. She has to care for a seven-year-old daughter and an aged mother-in-law. Polio deformed her right arm and leg. But Riasa has hope because of loans from one of David's partners. With her first loan of twenty-five dollars (U.S.) she bought corn and made small cakes to sell in the local market. From the profits she repaid that loan and then expanded her tiny business with a second fifty-dollar loan. Now repaying her third loan, she plans to open a small shop at the front of her tiny house.

From 1981–1993, David and his partners in the Opportunity Network made loans to forty-six thousand tiny entrepreneurs like Riasa and created 77,700 new jobs among the poor. Even when you include all related costs like consulting and training, each loan costs less than five hundred dollars, and the money gets paid back at reasonable interest within a year and then gets loaned again to empower another poor person and that person's whole family.

Seventy-seven thousand new jobs for the poor is an amazing achievement for a person who spent the first sixteen years of his life in an orphanage. He left without a cent, but in the next nineteen years he made a considerable amount of money. And then, after a few years when God reeducated him by having him live among the poorest in Asia, he used the next sixteen years to become one of the world's most successful bankers for the poor.

David does not know a thing about his parents. "For all I know, I may have been picked out of a garbage basket."[1] So he grew up in an Anglican orphanage of northern New Zealand, where life was tough. There was enough food and clothing plus solid practical training, but no emotional warmth. For all of the sixteen years in the orphanage, "no one ever showed me any love," David told me. David remembers cleaning a bully's shoes and making his bed. (Today he is not proud of the fact that he demanded the same of someone else!) He also remembers sneaking out at night to ride bikes and steal apples.

Somehow, in his loneliness—perhaps because he had absolutely nothing else to depend on—he developed a powerful sense of God as Father. This trust in the Heavenly Father that took deep root in the orphanage has continued as the foundation of his life. "Throughout my life, I've had a concept of God the Father that a lot of people don't have, because I can see how God has sustained me right from birth. I have a very strong feeling of God as a Father who really cares and who provides."

Orphanage rules required David to leave at age sixteen. So in 1956, he stepped out alone into the big world with absolutely nothing—no family, no close friends, no money. All he had was a belief in God and driving ambition. Somehow he managed to get a hot-dog stand. Within a couple months, this competitive sixteen-year-old had six other kids leasing hot-dog stands from him. With the capital they produced, David bought a little bakery and expanded its operations. When he sold the bakery, he purchased a biscuit factory—then a pancake restaurant and other small businesses.

He had never had any business training, but each business grew. So did David's capital.

When he was twenty-four, David met Carol Crowder, who had just graduated from college with a degree in education. Soon after their marriage eighteen months later, they decided to migrate to Australia. Carol was quite ill, and they hoped that better medical help there and a new environment would help. So they sold their businesses and moved.

In Australia, David started working for a man in the construction industry. He had no training in that field except for some elementary courses while at the orphanage, but he was soon a partner in the business. Not too much later he bought the man out and set up three different construction companies of his own. He also purchased a number of stores selling supplies to the construction industry. By 1974, his construction companies alone had over one hundred employees.

This New Zealand orphan was clearly a success. He had made his first million by the time he was thirty-five. Virtually everything he tried worked. "By that time, it was clear that I was an entrepreneur and whatever business I chose to take on, I was going to make a success of it."

David could have gone on to make more and more money for himself, but God had a different plan. God wanted to retrain him so he could make more and more money for others. On Christmas day, 1974, a devastating cyclone struck Darwin, a town on the far northern coast of Australia where many native Australians lived. David answered the S.O.S. of his church and took twenty employees up to Darwin to repair buildings for six weeks.

After his return, business as usual seemed to lose some of its attraction. Making more money no longer was appealing. David and Carol began to sense the Holy Spirit calling them to use their skills and resources "for the sake of the Kingdom and not just for the sake of making a profit." Discomfort with their affluent lifestyle began to grow. Slowly, they developed what they now call an "economics of enough." David explained, "Basically, there's a plateau or a level of capital that you need to survive and after that it becomes surplus and permits you to indulge."

There were no heavenly voices or miraculous signs. Just the

inner tugging of the Spirit. At no point in David's life, in fact, had there been any dramatic conversion. In spite of failures and sin here and there, he had always felt God's love and sought to follow Christ. David and Carol were active in their local church. In 1975, however, God was clearly inviting them to a major new step of discipleship.

They sold some of their businesses and put trusted managers in charge of the rest. The whole family moved to Darwin for a year. David supervised the stream of volunteer carpenters from all over Australia who came up to Darwin to help native Australians rebuild after the cyclone. Carol ran a local hostel.

Soon, another disaster prompted another move. When the 1975 earthquake devastated sections of Bali including the Christian village of Blimbingsari, the Bali church sent an S.O.S. to Australian Christians. It only took David and Carol a couple months to respond. They had no idea how dramatically this move would change their lives, but they were ready to go.

In December 1976, they packed their bags and moved their two young daughters, Natasha and Rachel, to the devastated rural village of Blimbingsari in Bali (see chapter 6). There were no roads, just a broad track through the jungle to the village. Carol home-schooled the girls. David organized numerous projects, built a dam, a church building, a bridge, a clinic, and irrigation systems. They paid their own expenses and even donated money to some of the projects.

David always brought a shrewd business eye to every setting, so it is not surprising that he soon noticed that even after basic infrastructure like roads, irrigation systems, and schools were in place, economic growth was slow. When he traveled to the very poor Hindu villages around the Christian village of Blimbingsari, he saw how the extreme poverty was related to a vicious debt cycle. Landless tenant farmers working other people's fields had to borrow money at outrageous rates during the season when they had no crops. David saw clearly how important it would be if these very poor people could have access to tiny amounts of capital at reasonable interest rates. "So we started loaning to individuals to help them out of this poverty cycle, and I guess that was the birth of the revolving-credit program that we set up in Bali."

David started making loans of twenty-five, fifty dollars, one hundred dollars, or three hundred dollars to very poor people. Each loan helped a very poor person get some simple tools and enough supplies to increase the family's income. Because it costs a bank almost as much to process a loan of one hundred dollars as it does to process a loan of ten thousand dollars, and the person who only needs one hundred has no property to back up the loan—the banks ignore the credit needs of the poorest. All the poor can do is go without or borrow from loan sharks at outrageous rates. A tiny loan, David discovered, brought new hope, dignity, and rapid growth in family income. Without fully realizing the implications, David had stumbled onto a crucial method to empower the poor.

After two years in Blimbingsari, the Bussaus returned to Australia to take care of their remaining businesses. But Wayan Mastra, leader of the Bali Protestant Church, invited them back in 1980. Dr. Mastra wanted to develop the fledgling center at Dhyana Pura into a viable self-supporting conference center. David turned it into a thriving business, added buildings, and created major income-generating programs for the church. He also helped develop a hotel-training program there.

Even more significant for the future, Mastra asked David to set up a solid development program for the church in Bali. The church had a small farm, but it was not very successful. So David brought in a young man called Priyadi Reksasiswaya to direct the program. David trained him, and together they set up a revolving-credit program to make tiny loans to poor people as he had done at Blimbingsari. In 1982, these programs directed by Priyadi became a separate church agency called MBM (see chapter six). Within a decade MBM had grown to be a multimillion dollar operation, transforming the lives of tens of thousands of poor Balinese. It had also helped inspire forty-seven similar agencies in nineteen other countries.

In 1981, the Bussau family again returned to Australia—this time because their daughters were ready for high school. They sold more of their businesses and set up the Maranatha Trust. Carol chose the biblical word *maranatha*[2] because she and David wanted to underline their desire to be good stewards of their resources until the Lord's return. Maranatha Trust is not a grant-making agency although occasionally it has given funds for specific programs. Rather, it provides the income and structure so that David can now volunteer his time to promote the kind of revolving-credit program he learned how to do in Bali.

Two special relationships have been especially important in the development of David's work. The first is the cooperation with Opportunity International, and the second is the partnership with Vinay Samuel (see chapter 3).

In 1980–81, Opportunity International (then called Institute for International Development) was trying to start several economic development programs including a revolving-credit scheme in Indonesia.[3] Everything flopped.

Fortunately, the director of the program in Indonesia took a vacation in Bali and met David. When he learned about the successful programs of David and the Bali church, he asked for help. David's assistance was so significant that when he completed these immediate projects, Opportunity decided that rather than run their own programs in Indonesia, they would simply fund the Bali church's MBM programs in revolving credit. As the Bali model expanded, the partnership deepened. Over the years, the close cooperation between Opportunity and David has brought together the funding and the expertise to develop the Opportunity Network. It now has forty-seven partners modeled on MBM in twenty-two countries in Asia, Africa, Latin America, and Eastern Europe.

The partnership between the Australian businessman David Bussau, and the Indian church leader and theologian Vinay Samuel, started in the United States. In the 1970s, a Philadelphia-based organization, Partnership in Mission, was trying to share the news about indigenous, wholistic models like the Bali church, which combined evangelism and social transformation in culturally appropriate ways. Vinay Samuel (see chapter three) was one of the younger leaders they identified who shared this vision. Through their work, David and Vinay met and quickly formed a very close friendship and extremely creative partnership. Vinay invited David to help set up a revolving-credit program in Bangalore in 1984.

In 1982, David attended an international consultation in Mexico called by Vinay and other Third World evangelicals. That meeting led to the influential International Fellowship of Evangelical Missions Theologians (INFEMIT). From the beginning, David has served as treasurer, and Maranatha Trust has facilitated the work of this important international network. Today, INFEMIT operates a publishing house, publishes an international journal, runs a program offering graduate degrees, and sponsors international conferences. Vinay's and David's deep trust and mutual intersection of gifts have greatly strengthened INFEMIT's impact on the worldwide church.[4]

Spreading the Model

The story of Titian Budi Luhur (TBL) on the Indonesian island of Sulawesi illustrates how the model David helped develop in Bali is rapidly spreading to other places. As the Balinese church in Sulawesi grew (see chapter six), they realized they needed the same kind of small-loans program and Rice Bank developed by MBM in Bali. MBM and David's Maranatha Trust agreed to help the Donggala church synod in Sulawesi set up their own program (TBL) in 1989. Opportunity helped provide capital. By 1994, three thousand two hundred small loans had been made and about two thousand farmers participated in the Rice Bank. About forty-five percent of the beneficiaries have been Christians; thirty-five percent, Muslims; and twenty percent, Hindus. The local churches have seen an increase in the regular giving of their members. By 1994, TBL had also helped establish three other partner agencies like itself in other parts of Sulawesi.

The Philippine partner that the Opportunity Network set up in 1980 has grown even faster. By the end of 1993, there were nine different Philippine partner agencies that had provided 8,675 loans. The international training center for the global network headed up by Dr. Ruth Callanta is also located in the Philippines.[5]

Larry and Josie Bueno make nuts and bolts.[6] They started in 1981 with ninety dollars of capital and a little space in front of their tiny house. But in 1987, they got a crucial loan for one thousand dollars from Opportunity's Philippine partner (TSPI) to buy a machine to mass-produce their product. A little later, another loan of thirty-two hundred dollars enabled them to buy more equipment and employ more workers. Two more additional loans from TSPI were also quickly repaid. By 1993, they had grown to a point where a major Philippine bank was glad to loan them money. By 1993, Larry and Josie Bueno employed twenty workers, providing them with good housing and Social Security benefits.

Much of David's time now goes into nurturing new partner agencies like MBM in Bali and TBL in Sulawesi. Forty-three partners existed by the end of 1993, and more emerge every year. David does not start new ones on his own. Existing partners play a central role in mentoring and training emerging partners. And David and the Opportunity Network are always there encouraging, advising, and inspiring.

Launching a new partner now starts with the identification and training of a small group of local business leaders who are committed Christians. David takes special joy in identifying such people and offering them a unique opportunity to use their business skills to serve Christ. "I have an empathy with the business community," he says. He put it gently, but David is annoyed that many successful Christian business leaders are in churches "who are not using their gifts and talents and skills." David has a solution for his and their frustration! He invites them to do "marketplace evangelism" making loans to the poor.

This first stage of finding the right strong, indigenous board members takes one to three years. Potential board members often go to a short session at the network's Center for Community Transformation in Manila. David believes in not rushing this process because he wants Christian business leaders who are both deeply concerned about the poor and eager to witness to Christ in the marketplace. "Basically, what I do now," David says, "is move around and walk alongside the boards of directors of these organizations. My ministry," he adds, "is to challenge successful Christian businessmen in developing countries to use the gifts and skills God has given them to help the poor. I guess it's because I went through that process myself that I can challenge them."

When the local board is ready, they hire an Executive Director and develop a pilot program of revolving credit that fits the local situation. but they draw on the experience and expertise of the entire Opportunity Network. If the pilot program works, the local partner and Opportunity enter upon a three- to five-year period of expansion. By the end of that time, the local partner is usually self-sufficient.

Initial funding for the project comes from the Opportunity donor network. Opportunity usually donates major funds only for about five years because they believe strongly in local self-sufficiency. Each loan includes a reasonable interest rate, and more than ninety-seven percent of all loans are repaid. Once each loan is repaid, the partner agency reloans the money to another person. Just like a bank, interest on the loans covers the operating costs. Every plan for a new partner is designed so that partner will become a self-sufficient, "mature" partner within a few years.

David likes to advertise the Opportunity programs as "the charity that doesn't give anything away." Everybody who receives a loan must pay it back at reasonable market rates. Every partner agency must learn how to manage its loan funds in order to pay its own way. The poor, David insists, need "a way out, not a handout." David promotes "profit, productivity and professionalism." He believes many aid groups have unfortunately fallen into the "triple-P syndrome" by looking down on profit, productivity, and professionalism. A columnist writing for the *Far Eastern Economic Review* probably got it right when he suggested that David Bussau is "something of a cross between John Wesley and Adam Smith."[7]

Every micro-loan starts with a recommendation by a respected community leader—often a Christian pastor or a Hindu or Muslim religious leader. Then the staff assist the entrepreneur with a business plan (even when they are illiterate). Staff also decide whether the person can increase their income by at least enough to sustain them and repay the loan. Before they receive a loan, most people also attend a "Value Formation Seminar" that teaches prospective loan recipients about ethics, integrity, stewardship, accountability, and concern for employees. They don't label it as Christian ethics, but the principles are biblical. Loan recipients also receive training on technical matters like inventory control, product marketing, and business growth.

Opportunity partners have a higher loan-repayment rate than many other agencies partly because they put more emphasis than most on supporting the person after the loan is made. During regular visits, a project officer sits down with each person and goes over the details of the business. They explore what is going well and where the person needs help. They also see these visits as a way to care personally for the individual as an expression of Christian love.

Mauj Masih grew up in a Muslim family of landless farmers in a poor village in Pakistan. The police collaborated with the landlords, who had no interest in seeing their laborers escape grinding poverty, illiteracy, and lack of health care. Fortunately, Mauj Masih heard about the small loans available through Alfalah Development Institute (ADI), an Opportunity partner established in Pakistan in 1986. An initial loan enabled him to start his own business—trading cattle. His success encouraged twenty-five other families to get loans so they could grow their own crops, raise livestock, and engage in a variety of small businesses. Life has changed dramatically in their poor community. Twenty of their children are now in school. Local landlords complain that cheap labor is no longer available because the poor villagers all have their own businesses. But they don't harass the poor anymore.

ADI in Pakistan is just one of forty-three independent partners The Opportunity Network has helped launch in Asia, Africa, Latin America, and Eastern Europe. Those partners now have eleven hundred staff and board members. The conscious intention was to establish autonomous, indigenous, self-supporting partners. "We have a principle not to own any of the organizations," David proudly reports. "Nothing is called Maranatha Trust." Each partner still shares quarterly reports with Opportunity support offices around the world. All the partners meet once a year for inspiration, biblical reflection, worship, sharing, and planning for expansion. But each local partner is an independent member of the larger "family."

One measure of the network's maturing is that country-wide

networks have emerged in Indonesia, the Philippines, and India. Priyadi Reksasiswaya, who managed the original model (MBM in Bali), now directs an Indonesian organization, DBB. DBB is controlled by the individual Indonesian partners, and its goal is to grow the model of revolving-credit programs by nurturing new partners in other parts of Indonesia. APPEND is the counterpart of DBB in the Philippines. Linking all the individual partners and countrywide networks in Asia is the Asia Partners in Development and its regular newsletter, *Asia News*.

The rapid growth of more and more independent partners does not mean that David has nothing to do. The Opportunity Network has thirty-two staff in support offices at Maranatha Trust in Australia, Opportunity International in the U.S. and elsewhere. David and his colleagues at Opportunity continue to walk alongside the other partners as friends and consultants, helping them locate resources and develop better programs.

The network has also recently set up Opportunity donor partners in England, Germany, New Zealand, and Canada. They also have plans for Switzerland and Sweden. They want to encourage Christian business leaders in other developed counties to raise funds to provide the capital for the ever-growing circle of partners running revolving-credit programs in the Third World. In fact, Western business leaders are very attracted to this program because every donation gets used again and again as it is reloaned every year.

You don't have to be a wealthy business leader to join David's worldwide ministry. For fifty dollars a month, you can, through the Opportunity network, make a loan to a tiny business person and stay in touch with that person as the business develops.[8] It's incredible, but true. Almost everyone who reads this chapter has the power to start or encourage a small business among the poor.

Do the tens of thousands of loans that David's partners are now making each year witness to Jesus Christ and help build the church? The answer is yes, although it is often not easy to demonstrate tight, exact connections. David can tell you precisely how many loans they have made at what average cost and how many jobs have been created among the poor. But it is not possible to offer any mathematical ratio between dollars invested and people converted.

David's deepest desire, however, is to witness to Jesus Christ, bring people to faith, and strengthen the church. Maranatha's mission statement declares that "in responding to the needs of poor non-Christians, we are extending God's love and fulfilling his commandment to witness to the Good News of the Kingdom of God come in Christ to redeem all people's relationships." They give loans to everyone (overall, sixty-seven percent now go to non-Christians) and rejoice when non-Christians experience economic benefits. But Maranatha insists that "they will fall short if they do not have Christ in their lives also." In a paper written in November, 1993, David points out that the largest number of both the poorest and the unevangelized are in Asia. Therefore, it concludes, "both evangelism and social concern are imperative.[9]

In 1993, Larry Reed, the African Regional Director, walked into their Zimbabwe office and found the staff members praying. So he sat down quietly and listened as the staff prayed with a woman who had asked how to become a Christian. Later, he learned that when the woman came for a loan, she asked why Zambuko Trust (that is the name of the Zimbabwe partner) made loans to poor people when nobody else would. The staff explained that it was because of Christ's love. Her response? She asked how she could become a Christian!

Zambuko Trust only got started in 1991. But by the end of 1993, it had already made about five hundred loans (three hundred went to women). In addition to creating two hundred new jobs, those loans have added power and credibility to the sharing of the Gospel.

None of the partners pressure anyone to accept Christ. In fact, a recent study by the University of Manchester reported that throughout the Maranatha network, they found "no evidence of aggressive or insensitive evangelism."[10] More than half of all loans go to non-Christians. But when people ask, David and his partners gladly share the Gospel. That's what they mean by "marketplace evangelism."

David believes there is "a greater need to witness in the marketplace than in the pews."[11] He believes that Christian business leaders engaged in revolving-credit programs for the poor have a special opportunity to witness to the Gospel.

The constitution of every partner agency explicitly identifies the organization as a Christian organization motivated by Christ to serve the poor. The board of directors and top staff are all Christians. Loan recipients all know that the program is Christian even though two-thirds of the loans now go to non-Christians. Not every project officer is a Christian, but eighty-five percent are. When the opportunity arises, they share the Gospel or refer people to a local pastor.

Indirectly, David's work definitely succeeds in accomplishing his desire to build stronger, economically self-sufficient local churches. When they loan to Christians, they teach biblical principles of stewardship and accountability and encourage the recipient to tithe. That enables the local church to be less dependent on outside funds. Loans to non-Christians made by an explicitly Christian organization add credibility to the words of local Christians even when there is no explicit evangelism in the loan program. In fact, some of the partners work in settings where direct evangelism is difficult or even legally forbidden.

David Bussau has come a long way since he walked out of that small New Zealand orphanage as a lonely, scared sixteen-year-old. He now has friends—both very wealthy business leaders and very poor men and women starting tiny businesses—all around the world. He has been one of the central leaders in the formation of one of the best global networks making loans to the poorest of the earth. His work strengthens the church and brings credibility to the Gospel in countries around the world. Ever modest, David would only want to be called a businessman who loves the Lord. The Lord has made him a pioneer marketplace evangelist and global banker for the poor.

---

1   Except where otherwise indicated, quotations come from personal interviews. David Bussau does not do self-promotion, so there is not very much material about him apart from the precisely accurate, readily available statistical/financial reports on the ministry. But *The Mango Tree Church* (see n. 1, chapter 6) has some material (especially chap. 8).

2   See 1 Corinthians 16:22. "Maranatha" means "Come, O Lord."

3 Another Christian businessman, Alfred A. Whittaker, played a key role in founding the Institute for International Development, which eventually became the American partner in the international Opportunity Network. Whittaker had been president of Bristol-Myers International and the Mennen Corporation before he decided, like David Bussau, to empower the poor rather than make more money.

4 For information on INFEMIT, write to P.O. Box 70, Oxford, England OX2 6HB.

5 See the forthcoming interview with Ruth Callanta in *Transformation* sometime in 1995.

6 See the 1992–1993 Annual Report, *Pushing the Frontiers,* available from Tulay Sa Pag-Unlad, Inc., P.O. Box 49, Greenhills, 1502 Metro Manila, 18–19.

7 William McGurn, October 14, 1993.

8 For Information, write to Opportunity Foundation, Ltd., P.O. Box 886, Bondi Junction, 2022, Australia, and ask for the address of their agency in your country that channels money to the Opportunity Network. In the U.S. write to Opportunity International, P.O. Box 3695, Oak Brook, Illinois, 60522.

9 "Maranatha Trust/Opportunity Programs: The Role of Enterprise Capital in Growing a Church" (Unpublished paper, November 1993), 8.

10 Quoted in William McGurn, "Missionary Capitalism," *The American Spectator,* December 1993, 35.

11 "Marantha Trust/Opportunity Programs," 2.

8

Athletes for Christ
in the Inner City

*God, I want you to know I will do anything
that you want me to do with my life.*

Wayne Gordon

Usually, affluent African-Americans move away from the ghetto. Carey and Melanie Casey did just the opposite.

Carey and Melanie had made it. Both had excellent jobs. Carey was an executive with the Fellowship of Christian Athletes. He was a chaplain for the U.S. Olympic team. NFL legends like Herschel Walker, Tom Landry, and Reggie White were good friends. Melanie had grown up in a middle-class black family who owned the only indoor swimming pool in their neighborhood.

In 1992, however, they sold their suburban house outside Kansas City, and moved to Chicago's North Lawndale, the fifteenth poorest neighborhood in the United States. The house next door was a center for drug dealers. Instead of quiet evenings by the fireplace, they suddenly struggled with nights full of blaring music, screams, and gunshots.[1]

Why? Why would anybody who had a choice move to a tough inner-city neighborhood where gangs, drugs, and murder stalk the streets? Sixty percent of the adults in North Lawndale never graduated from high school. Over fifty percent of the people are unemployed. Many of Carey and Melanie's friends—even their Christian friends—thought they were crazy. "We're battling a value system that tells us that success is the opposite of what we're doing."[2]

So why did the Caseys move? Because they believed God was calling them to minister in the inner city. And because they wanted to link arms with a white couple, Wayne and Anne Gordon, who had made the same move more than fifteen years earlier. That, too, had seemed crazy, but God had used Wayne and Anne to develop a fantastic church and community center in North Lawndale and Wayne wanted a strong, gifted black brother to be his co-pastor, peer, and colleague.

Lawndale Community Church is an amazing place. About five hundred people (black and white) worship there each Sunday. The church's outreach programs include a medical clinic with seventeen doctors who serve four thousand people each month. There are also programs in housing and education. By 1994, the annual budget was approximately seven million dollars. The church and many of the ministries operate out of a renovated building that formerly served as a warehouse for a used-car dealer who counted gangster Al Capone as a regular customer. More than one hundred people came to Christ last year through the many ministries of Lawndale Community Church. They have already planted a new church in a nearby Hispanic neighborhood.

It all started back in Iowa where a white kid named Wayne Gordon heard an unusual call from God. Wayne grew up in a Christian home. He had perfect church attendance for eight straight years but never surrendered his life to Christ until he attended a Fellowship of Christian Athletes summer camp after his sophomore year in high school. One night soon afterward, something unusual happened as Wayne lay in bed praying. "God," he said, "I want you to know I will do anything that you want me to do with my life."[3] Immediately, powerfully, although without hearing any audible sound, Wayne felt God respond: "I want you to work with black people." Wayne promptly thought of Africa, but God said, "No, it's right here."

It was one o'clock in the morning, but Wayne jumped out of bed to tell his mom and dad. In fact, he informed them he was supposed to quit high school the very next day and get started. Fortunately, they were able to help Wayne see that God would not object if he took a little more time for further preparation and study. So Wayne finished high school, went to Wheaton College, played football, and prepared to be a teacher and coach in the inner city.

Wayne had no idea how to get started. Then one day he heard

about a coach in an inner-city high school who had recently become a Christian in a Billy Graham crusade. Wayne went to Farragut High, looked up the coach, and landed a volunteer coaching job. Even though the city had a total freeze on hiring, Wayne had a full-time teaching job at Farragut High within four months.

Wayne's next move dumbfounded everyone. Not a single teacher at Farragut High—black or white—lived in the neighborhood. But, Wayne believed, God wanted *him* to live there so—against everyone's advice—he moved. Lawndale had lost half its housing since the 1950s when one hundred twenty-five thousand whites lived there. Vacant lots were everywhere. Eighty percent of the manufacturing firms (and jobs) had left. Decay, crime, and drugs ran wild. Martin Luther King, Jr., lived briefly in Lawndale in 1966 to dramatize the lack of jobs and housing. But God said, Move, so Wayne relocated in September 1975.

The second week he was there, Wayne started a Bible study for his high-school kids. Very quickly his apartment was full of kids almost every evening. Even more came when he found the money to buy a weight machine so the kids could work out every night in an old storefront near his apartment.

In June 1977, Wayne married Anne Starkey. The very first night they returned to Lawndale after their honeymoon, someone broke into their apartment. That happened again—in fact, nine more times—in the first three years of their marriage. Sometimes, Wayne remembers, he shook his fist at God and angrily demanded protection. Somehow they stuck it out. Fortunately, Anne shared Wayne's call, and together they persisted.

More and more students from Wayne's classes and sports teams at Farragut High crowded into their Bible clubs. Wayne and Anne shared their struggles, led them to Christ, and began the long task of discipling them, but they could not persuade them to go to any of the one hundred-fifty churches in Lawndale. Slowly they realized the kids needed a different kind of church for unchurched inner-city youth. The kids did not have money for Sunday clothes or church offerings, so they planned a church for kids in jeans and tennis shoes, without any offering.

On March 5, 1978, seven high-school kids plus Wayne, Anne,

and two other couples held the first service of what God would eventually grow into one of the most successful wholistic urban ministries in Chicago. Wayne's "relationship evangelism" was effective. "Every kid I know has scores of problems, frequently among them fractured families. . . . So you end up being a great friend and often a father image in many kid's lives." "Just being there and loving them unconditionally"[4] was powerful. More and more young people flocked into the first-floor storefront below the apartment where Wayne and Anne now lived. They lifted weights, played Ping-Pong, shared their dreams and struggles, studied the Bible, and on Sunday, worshiped together in the little one-room storefront. Wayne still taught and coached at Farragut High—to this day, they call him "Coach"—but he was now also the pastor of a small, growing congregation.

From the beginning, this little church tried to live out Jesus' second command to "love your neighbor as yourself." One day during its first year during which they had grown to fifteen, they drew up a list of needs in the community. All the thirty or forty items seemed overwhelming and far beyond their ability and resources. Then a mother who was afraid to go out at night to the neighborhood laundromat suggested that the church might install a washer and dryer in their storefront. A month later, a suburban family called. They had a perfectly good washer and dryer, they said, but the color of both was avocado—and they were changing the color scheme in their utility room! So they didn't want them anymore. Wayne picked them up, installed them in the church storefront, and opened their laundromat. Community ministries had begun.[5]

Today, those community ministries are a multi-million dollar complex of programs in health care, counseling, housing, education, and job creation. At the center of all these outreach programs, however, is an ever-expanding church. Wayne and Carey and all the other leaders insist that a wholistic approach is essential. People do need good housing, education, jobs. "But a health center will not save the city," Wayne insists. "Nor will giving everybody a job or a nice place to live. Long-term change is going to take a wholistic approach."[6]

That's why evangelism is central to everything done at

Lawndale Community Church (LCC). But not just any kind of evangelism. LCC practices "relationship evangelism."

An early unsuccessful evangelistic attempt has molded Wayne's approach. Stanley was a member of the first football team that Wayne coached. One night, over a pizza, Wayne tried to tell him that Jesus died for his sins. To Wayne's astonishment, Stanley *had* no sense of sin even though he was cheating on tests and sleeping with his girlfriend. Standard evangelical evangelistic techniques didn't work with Stanley.

Wayne began to realize that too often people are viewed as mere pawns to be won for Christ. Instead, he took Matthew 22:34 as a key and began to ask how he could love his needy neighbors the way Christ loved them. "So what we are doing here," Wayne says, "is motivated by evangelism, but evangelism is just one part of loving a person. Loving the total person is what we're striving to do. And that is motivated by our love for God. It's the great commandment and the second-greatest commandment."

That is the focus of every program at Lawndale. Whether it is the doctor in the medical clinic, the person managing the low-income housing, or the shepherding pastor, everyone seeks to love the whole person. "The church sort of puts their arms around the community," says Louie Winternheimer, one of the doctors in the clinic, "and says, 'Look, God loves you, and this is a practical way that we are going to show God's love.'" The various ministries are designed to offer ways to help Christians build relationships with non-Christians so they can help them become the whole persons God intended. Wayne has no patience with one-sided applications of the Gospel:

> If you have the spiritual gospel without the social gospel, you do not have the gospel. And if you have the social gospel without the spiritual gospel, you do not have the gospel. When I love my son and help him
> learn to read or give him food to eat, everybody says I am a great dad. But when I love the guy in the street, people say that is the social gospel. That is baloney! *The Gospel is for the whole person.* Proclaiming the Good News of Jesus Christ means taking care of people's needs physically, mentally, and socially, as well as spiritually.[7]

The organizational structure of LCC underlines the importance of the church in its wholistic theology. Lawndale believes the church must be at the center of genuinely Christian community development, so that's exactly where their flow chart places the church. The church names a Board of Deacons that works with Carey Casey, the Shepherding Pastor, to organize Sunday worship, discipleship, evangelism, and visitation. Financing for these programs comes from the Lawndale congregation. The church also names the Outreach Council that works with Wayne Gordon, the Outreach Pastor, to oversee the work in the community. Some of the outreach programs (including the medical clinic and the housing programs) operate under two separate legal entities, but at least a majority of the members of each board must be members of the church. Wayne serves as president of both boards. Most of the funding for outreach programs comes from outside Lawndale—from foundations, government, and other churches.

Ninety percent of LCC's one hundred-thirty staff members live in the Lawndale neighborhood and attend the church. Every morning, they gather in a circle at the beginning of the day to sing, worship, and pray together. I joined hands in this circle one morning recently when I was visiting. The devotional was not long, but their love for the Lord pulsated through the songs and prayer. Throughout the day, staff are always ready to talk or pray with anyone they sense has a spiritual need.

Regina Turner's attitude is typical of LCC staff. Regina has a busy job as receptionist for this vast operation. "Its real hectic here," Regina says, "but I'm working for the Lord." She has been there for nine years so everybody knows her—and many seek her advice and prayer. "They will call and ask to pray or just ask to talk. So its a ministry that I get paid for. I just come and work for the Lord and get paid." And when she hires other receptionists to help her, Regina makes sure that they are also seeking a ministry, not just a job.

Lawndale Christian Health Center

"Quality health care in an atmosphere of Christian love" is the slogan for the medical clinic. Started in 1984, the medical center served 30,800 different persons in the first eight years. By 1994, seventeen doctors were serving four thousand patients a month. An African-American who grew up in Lawndale is the full-time dentist. The clinic has an ophthalmologist, a large program for people with AIDS, and a program for uninsured children whose families are below the federal poverty level. Each year about twenty-five fourth-year medical students spend a month as interns at Lawndale, learning how Christian doctors can use their skills to serve the poor.

The health center is almost self-sufficient financially. Fees cover eighty five to ninety percent of its costs, but that is possible largely because the doctors work for one-third to one-half of what doctors normally earn. The city's public health department is amazed—they cannot find enough doctors even though they offer much higher salaries. Lawndale's doctors come and stay because they share Lawndale's wholistic vision. Seventy percent of the patients are on Medicaid. Only five percent have private insurance. Twenty to twenty-five percent pay on a sliding scale.

Anyone can receive care at the clinic. If they cannot afford the modest fee, they can work for twenty minutes. That approach applies to all LCC's ministries. To preserve dignity and avoid a welfare mentality, LCC hardly ever gives food, clothing, or services away for nothing. "We found," Gordon says, "that you don't give people anything. It strips people of their dignity. That's the problem with the American welfare system today."

People receive more than health care at the clinic. They also receive dignity, love, and personal affection. After the first visit, everyone sees his or her own private physician each time. Doctors are encouraged to build a personal relationship with each person they care for. Everyone from the doctors to the receptionists are committed Christians. They pray with patients, invite them to church, or refer them to the pastor.

Housing Programs

Decent, affordable housing is a desperate need in the inner city. Andy Krumsieg, who used to head up the housing programs, explains why a decent apartment or house is so crucial: "It gives people an oasis to go back to within the battlefield. We live in a war zone. If you have to go back and fight the roaches, the mice, the rats, and the plaster falling off the walls, and the electricity doesn't work and the plumbing leaks, you can't like going home. But when you have a decent house, it gives you an oasis to go back and rejuvenate."

Samaritan House provides temporary housing for homeless families. LCC's Development Corporation now owns and operates fifty rental apartments. A special rehab program enables Lawndale residents to help renovate vacant houses and become owners through a three-year lease/purchase arrangement. Another LCC housing program run in cooperation with developer Perry Bigelow enables Lawndale residents to invest seven hundred to one thousand hours of sweat equity in their future home. They actually go to the factory where the prehabbed homes are constructed and help build their own new three-bedroom house.

In a different program, Bigelow Homes and LCC are constructing seventy-two new townhouses. A twenty-thousand-dollar city subsidy for each makes them more affordable for Lawndale residents. In 1994, LCC launched a new three-million-dollar housing project.

Richard Townsell, who now serves as the Executive Director of the Lawndale Christian Development Corporation, is grateful for the impact of LCC on his life. He started at Lawndale as a teenager, wrestling in their athletics program and attending the Bible studies. At Northwestern University, he earned four varsity letters in wrestling. After university, he taught school for five years, and his wife became a chemical engineer at Amoco. But two years ago, this successful black couple chose to move back to Lawndale. Richard serves as a deacon in the church in addition to heading up the Development Corporation.

The impact of LCC's housing programs stares you in the face if you walk down Avers Street, just a couple blocks from LCC. It used to be one of the busiest drug streets in the city. One of the biggest drug busts in Chicago's history happened there in 1979. Then LCC bought and rehabbed two buildings on Avers Street from two convicted drug dealers, but everybody was afraid to move in. Finally Andy Krumsieg and his wife took the plunge. Since then, LCC has redone several other vacant buildings. The few home owners who had not left the block have also spruced up their houses, and the drug dealers and junk cars are gone. The change is so dramatic that the *Christian Science Monitor* ran a story on Avers Street (December 28, 1988).

People like Warren Lott help make LCC's work possible. Formerly a general contractor and the supervisor and technician for Honeywell in New Jersey, he took early retirement to become a full-time, volunteer maintenance man for LCC. Electrical work, plumbing, carpentry, whatever—Warren can do it.

If it were not for LCC's housing program, Precious Thomas would probably not be the Director of Education for LCC today. She grew up in Lawndale in the '50s when the neighborhood was overwhelmingly Jewish. In fact, she was one of only two or three blacks in the Lawndale schools at the time. For years, however, after graduating from college, she lived and taught school in the suburbs. Then, after a new experience with Christ, God called her back to Lawndale. Earlier, she says, "I just wanted to run away; that's why I was in the suburbs. I just wanted to get away from here completely because it was depressing. But now I don't feel that way. My goal in my heart is to reach out to young people and young minds."

Precious Thomas was ready to move back, but she wanted a decent place to live. Fortunately, one of LCC's newly rehabbed apartment units on Avers Street was available. A little later, she and her sister actually bought a building on Avers Street. Ms. Thomas is now back home in Lawndale directing several innovative educational programs.

Educational Ministries

LCC's Lawndale College Opportunity Program (LCOP) is a five-year college-prep program. They work with four local schools and select seventh-graders who come to LCC's Learning Center twice a week for help in math and reading. Volunteer tutors from Wheaton College come to help with math every Wednesday. Field trips, home visits, and one-on-one relationships with each student provide encouragement and incentive. So does the guaranteed college scholarship of three thousand per year for all who complete the program. Thus far, one hundred students have enrolled in LCOP, and eighteen have gone on to college.

Precious Thomas also directs the Lawndale Educational Advancement Program (LEAP) for kids from kindergarten to grade eight. These students come for two hours every day after school for help with homework, training on LCC's several dozen computers, Swahili classes, and Christian education. First Presbyterian of Glen Ellyn has provided some of the tutors for seven years. In this program, Wayne Gordon says, "you have every aspect of what we're trying to do to make a difference. You have black culture, you've got Christianity, you've got computers, a little something to eat, and time just to get yourself together."

Leadership Development

Discipling a new generation of African-American Christian leaders is at the heart of LCC's vision and program. This has been a special passion and gift of Wayne's over the years. A variety of youth programs, especially sports in the gym, have provided the opportunities for friendship and discipline. A full-size gym built with the help of a Chicago Bears' fundraiser resounds with the noise of a constant flow of recreational activities mixed with Bible study. Hundreds of kids play there every week. Assistant Pastor Vance Henry says the gym is a marvelous evangelistic tool because it provides a place to build relationships.

Randy Brown, the current gym director, first got in touch with LCC because its high-school outreach ministry was the only place in Lawndale where you could lift weights at night. At first he accepted the Bible study each evening as an unavoidable nuisance. Soon, however, Randy started attending church, and later he became a Christian. Now he devotes his life to helping the next generation discover the same joy and wholeness through the gym.

Walter Moore is another example of LCC's successful discipling of young African-American leaders. Walter grew up in Lawndale and met "Coach Gordy" when he was only eight. While a sophomore in high school, he accepted Christ through LCC's very active chapter of Fellowship of Christian Athletes. With scholarship help from the church, Walter attended Taylor University. During the summer, an LCC scholarship enabled him to come home and work in the Bible Vacation program. He also participated in the church's leadership-development program for African-American youth. At graduation, Walter was offered a great job with a major company. LCC also offered him a job as youth pastor. Walter was torn. His decision was wrenching. All through Taylor, he had lectured others on the importance of urban ministry, but he did not want to go himself. "I wanted to be as far away from Lawndale as I could possibly be. I knew what Lawndale was all about."

But God was calling Walter just as he had called Wayne Gordon and Precious Thomas. Just as he was struggling with his decision, Walter learned that the close friend of his younger brother back in Lawndale had been killed because he was dealing drugs. Walter decided he must return to help his little brother and the rest of his friends. So Walter came home to Lawndale's drug-infested streets. As youth pastor, he now heads up the Fellowship of Christian Athletes Program (an outreach program for non-Christians) and the high-school youth group (a discipling program for Christians). In the first two years after Walter returned in the fall of 1990, thirty-two kids accepted Christ through his FCA work. Many of them went on to college. Walter Moore demonstrates to inner-city skeptics not only that inner-city kids can escape the ghetto's terror but also that they can return to rebuild the city.

That kind of success does not came easily. Wayne remembers that the first ten Lawndale students he helped go on to college failed to graduate. Slowly, LCC learned how to support them even while they were away studying. Over fifty youth from LCC have graduated from college in the last ten years, and more than half have returned to Lawndale to serve. That is effective urban- leadership development. Only when you recall the setting, do you realize how stunning this record is. Fifteen years ago, hardly any Lawndale residents went to college, and the handful who did certainly did not return. But God is calling educated, dedicated Christian youth to return home to rebuild Lawndale.

One of the amazing things about LCC is that a white person could be so successful in an all-black neighborhood. That was possible only because of Gordon's sense of call, his readiness to relocate and raise his family in the community, his careful attention to learning more about African-American culture, his constant efforts to bring in visiting black leaders, and his attention to leadership development of community people.

God has worked through LCC to transform the lives of hundreds of people in North Lawndale. But it is always a struggle—sometimes, as the story of Stanley Ratliff indicates, a long, frequently disappointing struggle.

Stanley was one of the first guys Wayne coached. In fact, Stanley was there when Wayne first talked about moving into the neighborhood. Stanley's advice was blunt: "Coach, you can't live here. There ain't no white folks in this neighborhood." But Wayne moved, and Stanley joined his first Fellowship of Christian Athletes group for a year and a half. Then he went off to college and studied on and off for seven years. Even when he returned to the neighborhood, he did not attend Lawndale church.

But when he got in trouble with the law in the late '80s, he looked up his old coach for help. A friend had given Stanley a bag of cocaine to deliver. Stanley did not know what it was, but that did not help him with the law when the police arrested him. As Stanley spilled out his troubles, Wayne urged him to come to church the next Sunday. He came, and to his surprise he saw a couple other guys from the old Farragut High football team of fifteen years ago. Wayne, Stanley, and two of his old football buddies started meeting for Bible study at 6:30 A.M. Things seemed to pick up, and Stanley found a better job. But then his trial date arrived and the judge imposed a nine-year jail term. Wayne supported him in prison, and the church wrote him letters. While in prison Stanley completed his bachelor's degree, led a music group, and played in a rhythm-and-blues band.

In 1992 the governor of Illinois pardoned Stanley. To celebrate his release, the church welcomed him home with a special service, singing songs he had written in prison. Two of his friends who attended that unusual service were so struck by the love they saw that they accepted Christ. Today, Stanley is active in LCC's music ministry, playing, singing, and writing songs. His wife, mother, and several cousins also attend Lawndale. And Stanley often goes along to do special music when Wayne speaks in other churches.

Stanley's story has a happy ending, but it took several years, uncommon struggle, and great persistence to be Christ's channel of healing grace for Stanley. Obeying the Great Commission in the inner city is not for the fainthearted and impatient.

The coming of Carey Casey in 1992 as Shepherding Pastor represented a dramatic, courageous step for everyone. For over fifteen years Wayne had been the central leader, but Wayne increasingly felt overwhelmed as both pastor of a rapidly grow-ing congregation and head of a multimillion dollar, expanding community center. The shepherding of young black leaders—so central to Lawndale's mission—was not receiving enough atten-tion. And some community people thought, Wayne says, that "this white boy can't trust a black to run the ship."[8] So they decid-ed to call Carey Casey as co-leader of LCC. Many wondered, how-ever, whether a new black leader could work well with the white founder whom everyone called "Coach." It certainly would have been impossible if Carey had not been a strong person, but Carey Casey is a tall, self-confident, powerful black leader. Most morn-ings, Carey and Wayne meet at six for an hour of prayer and shar-ing. They thrash out misunderstandings and hurts as fast as they arise. They have built a strong friendship over the last two years that provides an inspiring model for the rest of the interracial congregation.

Carey and Wayne and their families know God has called them to North Lawndale. They also know the cost of their com-mitment. It was a frightening move for the three Casey children. "Every day we walk out our door," Carey says, "we put into prac-tice our belief that God is our protector."[9] While at Lawndale for a two-day conference recently, I listened to Wayne Gordon share the struggles of his young white son in an all-black neighborhood. "It's a lot tougher for me than for you, Dad," Andrew told his dad one night recently. The next day, Wayne left our meeting for awhile. When he returned, he told us he had been to Andrew's school because Andrew had been in a fight. LCC's amazing programs would not have developed if a few leaders like Wayne and Anne, Carey, and Melanie had not listened to God's call to relocate. Theirs has been a costly obedience.

Not everyone, of course, needs to move to the inner city. Many suburban Christians help make Lawndale work. Wheaton College students and members of Glen Ellyn Presbyterian help tutor students. Willow Creek and Christ Church of Oak Brook donate food. A number of suburban churches support LCC through their annual mission budget. Suburban Glen Ellyn Presbyterian Church celebrated their sixtieth anniversary in an unusual way. Instead of spending a great deal of money on themselves, they donated forty thousand dollars plus a considerable amount of volunteer labor to help LCC renovate its new Learning Center, where Precious Thomas now teaches scores of inner-city kids to use computers, speak Swahili, and understand the Bible.

LCC is wholistic mission at its best. LCC's staff lead scores of people to Christ every year. They also work hard to offer decent housing, jobs, affordable health care, and educational opportunity. And the different programs are so intertwined that it would be impossible to say with precision what is evangelism and what is social action.

Vanessa Little's story illustrates how it all fits together. She first came in contact with LCC through her brother, who was in one of Wayne's early FCA groups. When her brother got into trouble, the church's help astounded her. "I had never seen people reach out to help people like that." She began to attend church and soon became a Christian.

Vanessa now works at LCC's clinic. She and her husband William live on Avers Street in one of the houses remodeled by LCC. "We are going to own it in about thirty days," she proudly told a friend of mine.

Vanessa and William's oldest son graduated from college in 1993. LCC's youth pastor helped him choose a school and fill out the forms. Their fifteen-year-old son Kenneth is now in LCC's preparation program.

Transformed lives and a revitalized neighborhood through people who live as well as preach the Gospel—that's what Lawndale Community Church is all about. And that's why a white athlete from Iowa and a suburban black athlete from Kansas City would not want to be anywhere else than in the heart of inner-city Chicago.

1   See Andres Tapia, "We're Not in Kansas City Anymore," *Marriage Partnership*, Summer 1993, 44–49.

2   Quoted in ibid., 49.

3   Unless otherwise indicated, all quotations are from personal interviews.

4   "I'm Available Because I'm Always Here: A Conversation with Wayne Gordon," *Youth Worker*, Winter 1989, 77.

5   "Seekers or Saints," *Leadership*, Fall 1991, 21.

6   Wayne Gordon, "The Role of the Church in Community Development," in David Caes, ed., *Caring for the Least of These* (Scottsdale: Herald Press, 1992), 87.

7   Ibid., 83–84.

8   Quoted from "Passing on the Power," *Christianity Today*, October 4, 1993, 21.

9   *Marriage Partnership*, 49.

9

Combining Mass Evangelism and Social Action in a Secular Society

If anyone else but Jesus had preached that sermon in Matthew 25,
they'd be slung out of the church.

Steve Chalke

Steve Chalke flunked his exams. In fact, he flunked his exams several times. Today, he is the premier youth evangelist in England. His staff of seventy-five use state-of-the-art media technology, secular TV programs, scores of short-term youth teams and a number of social ministries to communicate the Gospel to secular Britain.

Steve's early years growing up in London were not easy. Racism prevented his Anglo-Indian father from getting a good job, even though, Steve says, "he had the qualifications to be headmaster of a school." Instead, he worked as a porter on British Rail. Steve used to lie awake at night, worrying that his dad might get beaten up on the night shift. At age eleven, Steve failed the exams that would have enabled him to go to one of the good academic schools, so he went to a dumpy secondary school where the kids beat up anybody who passed exams!

Steve attended a Baptist church with his parents, but he was always somewhat rebellious. One evening, while attending a concert by Graham Kendrick, Steve accepted Christ. He was only fourteen, but he knew that night that he wanted to spend the rest of his life preaching. At the same time, he began to dream of running a youth hostel, a hospital, and a school for the poor and homeless in inner-city London. When he was sixteen, he joined a small Christian band doing weekend evangelistic concerts. By sixteen, his sense that he was supposed to work in the city had grown very strong. He could see that the church thrived in the suburbs and the country but fell apart in the city. Steve felt God telling him to prepare to be a city minister who would preach and care for the poor and homeless.

But the Baptist Church said a minister had to be educated. That meant that Steve must pass the A-level exams so he could go to the Baptist Theological School, Spurgeon's College. So Steve went to a new school at sixteen to study for A-levels. It was only then that he realized how badly cheated he had been in his previous education. In the atrocious schools he had attended, he had not learned to think or write. At the end of two years, he failed the exam! His minister told him he would never get into Spurgeon's College. But Steve was determined. In four weeks of furious study on his own, he managed to master the material necessary to pass the A-level exam in religious education. He was ready for Spurgeon's!

The college, however, insisted that first he spend a year in a local church at Gravesend in Kent. During that year, Steve was depressed. He knew he earnestly wanted to be a minister, but everyone told him he had to have a "special call," and Steve didn't think he had one. Somehow, his inner sense of direction and longing did not seem like the call that everybody talked about. One day, he visited an old woman just three weeks before he was supposed to go to Spurgeon's. He was frantic because he knew they would ask about his "call." While the woman was making him some tea in the kitchen, he spied a book on her shelf with the title, *My Call to Preach*. Desperate, he reached for the book, thinking that he might find someone else's call and pretend that it was his own. He soon stumbled upon the "call" of a former principal at Spurgeon's. What he read left him dumbfounded. "I have never had a call to preach," wrote the former principal, "I just knew I had to do it from the day I became a Christian."[1] Steve was so relieved that he ripped the page out of the book and took it along to Spurgeon's! Today, Steve insists that God's call comes not necessarily through some special dramatic event but from the energy, enthusiasm, and drive that "God burns into you."

All through theological school, Steve talked about his desire to minister in the city, but when he graduated in 1981, a prominent suburban church in Tonbridge, Kent invited him to be their youth pastor. Steve struggled, but the principal suggested that this big church could help him in the future when he became a city minister. So Steve went to Tonbridge, and that's exactly what happened.

His four years as a youth minister in Kent were a dramatic success. The nationally famous Christmas Cracker program (which by 1993 had raised over 2.3 million pounds for Third World development) started there as a Christmas project in his youth group. One Christmas season, Steve learned from TEAR FUND about the need to drill wells in a drought-stricken area of India. Each well cost a thousand pounds ($1,500). The Tonbridge youth group was not really interested, but Steve persuaded these bored, Bible-belt, suburban kids to dream about ways to raise money. They hit upon the idea of a Beggars' Banquet—they would run a temporary restaurant selling inexpensive Third World meals at British prices. "Eat less and pay more" was the slogan. Fired up, the kids did everything, locating a shop, preparing the food, and publicizing the project. They cleared at least five thousand pounds. That was the beginning of what would become the biggest fund-raising project by Christian youth in all of England.

Developing new, relevant ways to challenge youth and to share the Gospel were Steve's special gifts. Gradually he started doing youth evangelism for all the churches of Kent. Then the Baptist Union in Great Britain encouraged him to develop a national ministry of preaching and teaching. The Tonbridge church offered to provide his salary, and church members helped set up Oasis Trust in 1985.

Reviving the Baptist church in Paddington was one of Oasis's early successes. In 1900, that church had one thousand members. In 1987, there were sixteen elderly folk left. The neighborhood was full of drugs, high-rise government housing, and unemployed adults. Steve invited six eighteen- to twenty-one-year-olds whom he had met in his preaching around England to come to Paddington and work with its new minister. Steve promised to train them one day a week as they worked in evangelism and social ministry in the community. The youth team spoke in the schools, ran youth clubs, knocked door-to-door in the housing blocks, and started a program for the unemployed in the community center. Sixty people accepted Christ that year and the church started to grow. Not surprisingly, the word spread quickly. Nine other churches asked for youth teams the next year. That was the beginning of Frontline Teams that by 1994 had over one hundred different teams serving in various parts of the world.

The story of Nikki illustrates Steve's unusual skill in calling out the gifts of young people. Nikki was a very unhappy member of Steve's youth group at Tonbridge. When her Christian parents separated, Nikki was so devastated that she dropped out of school. Steve needed a secretary to help with the new Oasis Trust so he hired this troubled seventeen-year-old. At times, Steve thought it just would not work, but Nikki grew, overcame her problems, and organized the office superbly. She has been a leader in several pioneer Oasis programs. Today, Steve says, she is one of the most experienced and gifted youth workers in England.

Oasis Trust found an inner city location for its expanding offices in a fascinating way. London has 278 Baptist churches, half of them, Steve says, "dead as doornails." One of them was Haddon Hall Baptist in a poor section of London. The name came from the great nineteenth-century Baptist preacher and theologian, Charles Haddon Spurgeon. It was one of the first churches he planted in London. By the mid-1980s, there were only five or six elderly folk left. On Sunday mornings, for one hour, they huddled on one pew at the front of a huge old building, but they had money at the bank, so they asked Oasis for a youth team. It was a disaster! Young and old could not agree on a significant strategy for ministry. "If you're going to go into church resurrection," Steve quips, "you've got to make sure the body is dead."

Steve refused to send another team unless things changed, but he did make them an offer. If they would donate the church's office space to Oasis for its headquarters, he would volunteer to be the pastor and lead the church without taking any salary. They agreed, and Steve was delighted because he had always felt drawn to pastor in the inner city. Another Frontline team of youth joined him to do the same combination of evangelism and social ministry that had revived Paddington Baptist. Neighborhood people came to church, and the church started to grow. Within three and a half years, average attendance was over one hundred, and the congregation was planning to start a new church down the road. Oasis, in the meantime, enjoyed very inexpensive office space.

Oasis's ministries are growing at a breathtaking pace. By 1994, their seventy-five staff supervised a vast range of programs. Oasis reflects the dynamic energy and creative flexibility of its young, thirty-eight-year-old leader. Structure never prevents Steve from listening to a gifted young person with a new idea. They flock to Oasis, which helps them implement their dreams. Remembering his own struggle with the notion of a call, Steve says "a call is energy and enthusiasm, a drive, that God puts in you, burns into you. It's what you're concerned about. You can't put it down. So we want to facilitate everybody in that. People are always ringing up Oasis." Money is usually tight and the salaries are modest. But youthful enthusiasm and a creative passion to make the Gospel relevant to secular Britain has created a powerful, dynamic ministry.

Oasis Trust now has four areas of outreach: communication, social care, training, and media. In addition, Oasis manages Christmas Cracker, which is now a separate organization.

Christmas Cracker has been Oasis's most visible program. The name came from a uniquely British Christmas present called "the Christmas cracker." It is a small gift that goes bang when two people tug on its two ends. Then a small trinket falls out. In 1987, while flying home from India, Steve thought up the idea of turning the Beggars' Banquet, which he had started at the Tonbridge church, into a national event. So he used one of his regular columns in a Christian magazine to describe how any youth group could organize a similar event in their area. The response astounded everyone. Today hundreds of youth groups run this type of restaurant for several weeks every Christmas.[2] Christmas Cracker is now the largest fundraising event by Christian youth in England. It has also spread to Australia and New Zealand.

Christmas Cracker does more than raise a lot of money for economic development in the Third World. It provides an opportunity to share a global vision with Christian youth. It strengthens the spiritual life of young Christians as they put their faith into action. It provides leadership training for Christian youth, many of whom have gone on to other Oasis programs. And it provides an unusual evangelistic opportunity. Christmas Cracker attracts a vast amount of attention in secular newspapers, radio, and TV. Many non-Christian youth sense the excitement and join in the fun and work. In the process, they become friends with Christian youth and catch a new sense of vital Christianity. Many have become Christians as a result of their involvement in Christmas Cracker.

Communication. Communication is Oasis's word for "evangelism." Oasis tries to figure out how to break through the boredom and misperceptions that block secular folk from truly hearing the Gospel. They also seek to use the secular media to share the Gospel. Since many non-Christians feel uneasy about the word *evangelism,* Oasis prefers the word *communication.* But their communication department is not focused on public relations and promotion! It's their evangelism division.

Oasis seeks to identify specific "people groups"—whether youth, prostitutes, the homeless—and ask how they can share the Gospel with them in culturally relevant, exciting ways.

Steve believes people are bored with the church but still interested in Jesus. "I get out and preach in churches and I'm bored. I sit there thinking, 'I wouldn't come here. It's irrelevant.' But people are interested in Jesus." So Oasis pushes the boundaries using high-tech video walls, secular songs, drama, and secular media to grab the attention of groups the churches are missing. They are constantly asking: What does it mean to speak the language of the youth, the homeless?

Oasis pioneered lively Christian video shows, but cheaper projectors soon meant that many local churches were also offering good presentations. So Oasis moved on to the video wall. Sixteen different TV screens linked by computers presented a fast-moving show. Oasis's Mercedes truck packed with equipment is an expensive £70,000 tool. But the state-of-the-art video presentation attracts youth.

Older folk also like their combination of technology, theater, and the Gospel. Oasis often presents "dinner and cabaret"-type evenings for adults. A local church does the dinner, and Oasis puts on a two-hour show of entertainment and bridge-building. They aim at an evening that is not "cringe-worthy." They want church members to be able to invite non-Christians to an evening during which the guests will feel comfortable. Music and videos from the '60s and '70s remind adults of the past. Then the show moves to the question: "That was then, but where are you now?" By the end, Oasis has shared Jesus in a fast-moving, enjoyable evening.

Some people criticize Oasis's approach. But Simon Parish, who heads up their communication department, says, "If we're going to be on the cutting edge of evangelism, then we have to be where people are at." And people today, both youth and adults, watch TV and attend high-class tech events. "You can no longer afford to do something that is nonprofessional, amateurish—you know, a slide projector and a couple slides on someone's trip to Afghanistan." Steve's response to those who say they can't use secular songs and a video presentation is simple: "Who says you can't? By all means, save some. Speak their language, get alongside them."

Oasis does eight to ten city-wide missions every year. Some are primarily for young people. Others are for all ages. For Festival '92 in Leeds, three hundred churches invited Oasis to do the youth component of a large city-wide mission. Lunchtime concerts and presentations in school assemblies by the drama group and video wall attracted young people to the evening events. Six or seven thousand heard their presentations and over two hundred made a commitment to Christ.

In evening events, Oasis uses all its techniques of drama and technology to give young people an exciting time, but in the last twenty-five minutes, Steve presents the Gospel very clearly. And he invites people to respond. There's no hype or pressure. "Look, if you want to make a decision, that's fine. But if you don't mean business with God, for goodness sake sit down. Don't stand up just because your friends are standing up."

Advance preparation and careful follow-up are important to Oasis for two reasons. First, because they want lasting change. And second, because the opportunity to come alongside local churches and offer training is almost as important as the immediate evangelistic impact of a mission.

Oasis works for up to eighteen months before a mission helping local churches prepare for follow-up. They train counselors, plan specific follow-up programs, and prod local churches to ask how much they may have to change if a large group of newly converted, unchurched kids flock into their meetings.

Oasis also makes sure the follow-up for youth is lively and fun. "There's a world of difference between how you follow up young people as opposed to older people," says Simon Parish. One church held its first follow-up to a mission at the local McDonald's. They rented the top floor, offered free burgers, and talked about Christian discipleship. Oasis helps local churches arrange follow-up events for youth so they can see that "Christianity is fun. You know, you've got the pool table, the table tennis and all that." But prayer and Bible study are also there. Oasis refuses to do missions unless the local church agrees to plan meaningful, relevant follow-up.

The story of Susan illustrates Oasis's belief that their weeklong mission should aim at training Christians as well as bringing non-Christians to faith. Susan[3] was the central leader of the Leicester University Christian Union. (The Christian Unions are the British equivalent of InterVarsity Christian Fellowship campus groups.) After Susan's Christian Union invited Oasis to do a mission at the university, Susan decided to prepare herself by taking Oasis's two-week training program in evangelism called Feet First. She participated enthusiastically in all the planning and events of the mission at Leicester University and then chose to spend a year in one of Oasis's Frontline Teams. Enthusiasm for evangelism and mission is now central to her life.

Heather Evans runs Oasis's "Capital Radiate." The two hundred-seventy Baptist churches of London have asked Oasis to train and mobilize their youth for evangelism. In the summer of 1992, they operated more than thirty outreach cafes—nonalcoholic bars that ran for one or two weeks, offering Christian bands and videos.

During Christmas, 1991, Oasis mobilized about two thousand churches across the country to share Christ through their program called "Christmas Unwrapped." Most Christians stick with their families and friends at Christmas and fail to use this public holiday about Jesus to tell others about him. Oasis designed a national advertising strategy. Cliff Richard, England's most famous pop-singer (and a committed Christian) recorded a special song that hit the top of the charts. Leaflets, posters, mugs, T-shirts, plus widespread coverage on secular radio, TV, and newspapers attracted a lot of attention. The purpose of this national visibility was to enable local churches to develop low-key, "carols and mince pie" evangelistic evenings. They hoped secular folk would say, "Hey, I saw something on TV about Christmas Unwrapped. This must be something big"—and then decide to accept an invitation from a neighbor to a local church's specially designed Christmas event for non-Christians.

On Fire is undoubtedly Oasis's most visible, most ambitious evangelistic venture. At Pentecost (May 21), 1994, over fifteen hundred churches and virtually all the denominations joined together in a "national birthday party for the church." There were celebrations of all kinds—fireworks displays, carnivals, dinner parties, street parties. A long list of fun events enabled Christians across the nation to explain the church's birthday so non-Christians could understand who they are and why they are celebrating. A major TV broadcast the next day attracted many viewers with its carnival atmosphere and stories about how Christian faith makes a practical difference in their daily lives. During two weeks of follow-up events, local churches sponsored a wide variety of evangelistic events and service projects that helped the community understand the whole gospel.

Oasis dreamed up the idea, but a wide cross-section of British Christians joined in the celebration. The list is very comprehensive: the Archbishop of Canterbury; many denominations including the Anglicans, Methodists, Baptists, Pentecostals, and Assemblies of God; black churches and house churches; virtually all the parachurch organizations. Very few Christian projects in England in recent years have united so many different Christians to share Christ. On Fire's combination of massive secular-media coverage, joyful public celebrations, local activity, service projects, and ecumenical participation make it a striking advance beyond the successful evangelistic crusades of Billy Graham and Luis Palau. That Oasis could conceive and manage such a project in a way that effectively attracted genuine ownership and participation by so many different Christian groups is a striking measure of Oasis's maturity, acceptance and skill. It is also, as Steve insists, a divine miracle.

Social Care. Steve has little patience with Christians who fail to serve their neighbors' physical needs. Matthew 25, he insists, means that "the result of being born again is that you will feed the hungry, give drink to the thirsty, and visit the prisoners, and if you don't you were never 'born again' in the first place." Steve adds that "if anyone else but Jesus had preached that sermon in Matthew 25, they'd be slung out of the Church!"[4]

In fact, Steve once turned down a million pounds ($1,500,000) because the donors demanded that he give up his social ministries. A few years after Steve's gifts as a youth evangelist became clear, a large trust with one million pounds offered to merge with Oasis. But there was one proviso attached to the huge grant: "We cannot have you investing it in social care. That is the job of the social workers. We are an evangelistic organization." Steve refused. "If you preach and you're not committed to real people," Steve replied, "then your preaching is not valid." Steve never got the money.

From the time he was a teenager, Steve dreamed of running an inner-city youth hostel for some of the thousands of poor, abused kids who flock to London looking for a better life. Tragically, they often end up on drugs, or in prostitution, or jobless, homeless, and sleeping on the streets. One day, a Christian offered to donate a very nice facility to Oasis for a youth hostel, but it was in a lovely suburb, not the inner city. Steve said no! The donor was shocked but so impressed with Steve's commitment that he returned a few days later. He offered to sell the property and give Steve the money. The total figure turned out to be one hundred-ninety-three thousand pounds. Oasis then purchased a large building in a poor section of London called Peckham and started the hostel. Today, No. 3, as it is called, serves about twenty to twenty-five troubled youth each year. They provide an apartment, training in budgeting, cooking, cleaning, and job-hunting, plus regular informal counseling.

It is striking that direct evangelism is so small a part of life at No. 3. All the staff are Christians. Occasionally, a resident comes to faith, but the staff do not organize any formal Christian activities. "Because we are not explicitly preaching to people, we're not explicitly getting a response," says Graham Mungeam, Oasis's chief executive. "Maybe we should be," he adds, "but we haven't been."

A medical center for the homeless was central to Steve's teenage dreams. It became a reality in June 1993 when the Elizabeth Baxter Health Center opened. Access to British health care begins with registration with a general practitioner. Unfortunately, many of the homeless are unregistered. Consequently, they often cannot take advantage of Britain's health-care services provided by the government. In Oasis's new facility, Christian staff offer a wide range of medical services to the homeless of London.

Dozens of Oasis's volunteers use a converted double-decker bus three nights a week to serve London's homeless. Homeless folk receive clothes, coffee, referral to some hostel for the homeless, and sometimes a sandwich. Mostly though, they discover people who care about them and gladly listen to their sad stories. The ultimate goal is to share the Gospel, but the evangelism is very low-key. Lisa Bugge has volunteered for some time with the bus's street teams. It's easier, Lisa admits, just to listen to their stories and not take advantage of the openings to share the Gospel.

It is interesting to reflect on Steve's theology of evangelism and social transformation in light of the apparent low level of personal conversions in Oasis's social ministries. Steve thinks that talking about evangelism and social concern as two blades of a scissors is "a load of old rubbish. I think they're both the same blade." If you go through the Gospel, Steve adds, you cannot say that in one passage Jesus is being evangelistic and in another that He is following his social-care policy. In Jesus, "it was all mixed up and jumbled up."

Steve admits that even Oasis makes the distinction. The communication department (evangelism) is separate from the social-care department. "But the distinctions are there just for administrative purposes." But maybe the administrative division in Oasis points to a point that gets blurred when we insist that evangelism and social concern are identical. They certainly are so mixed together that in practice they are often inseparable. Perhaps acknowledging that they are both distinct and inseparably interrelated helps us affirm the importance of both in a way that enables us to ask whether they are both present in a properly balanced way. Then one could ask whether it might be possible to integrate more consciously evangelistic activities into Oasis's social-care programs in ways that other ministries like Rock/Circle and Lawndale have done so successfully.

However we settle the question of language, it is abundantly clear that Steve is passionately committed to leading people to faith in Jesus Christ. And he is also deeply concerned to minister to the whole person. That is clear in all Oasis's work, including their training programs.

Training. Oasis has had brilliant success in training young people to share Christ's love in relevant ways with the whole person. A wide variety of programs combine teaching with practical, on-site learning. Steve thinks sermons without help in practical implementation are almost useless. "I have had sermons rammed down my throat. I've had them by the lorry load," Steve complains. "If sermons were going to change the world, we'd be living in utopia right now. But sermons don't change a thing until you do something. And when you do something, you learn." So Oasis works with local churches to develop practical, down-to-earth training programs that combine theory and experience.

Feet First is a short, two-week training program in evangelism for young people. The average age is nineteen to twenty. After five days of training, the youth hit the streets or the beaches with multimedia presentations, non-alcoholic bars, or street theater. Every team works with a local church that helps with planning and oversees follow-up. By 1994, about one thousand youth had gone through this powerful two-week program.

Oasis is grateful for every conversion and there have been many, but their first goal in Feet First is motivating and training young Christians. Feet First is designed for Christian youth—"to get their feet wet" in evangelism. And it works. Julian[5] was working in a secular job and struggling with many things when he joined Steve in a Feet First program several years ago.[6] Those two weeks changed his life. He soon joined a Frontline Team for a year. After that, he became a youth pastor and then enrolled at Spurgeon's College to train for the pastorate.

Frontline Teams is a one-year training program in wholistic mission for young Christians. By 1994, over four hundred youth (eighteen- to thirty-year-olds) had served in approximately seventy different churches. In 1994 alone, there were seventy Frontline team members in the UK and twenty-nine in other countries (including India and Tanzania). Participants value the learning experience so much that they raise most of the money for the year. Youth love the challenge that moves them from a comfortable Christianity that says "take up your cushion" for a risky venture that genuinely calls for taking up the cross. Local churches welcome the team because they provide youthful enthusiasm, energy, and additional arms and legs to get things done. Most of the teams go to city congregations where the lack of people to do ministry is especially desperate.

As the stories of Paddington and Haddon Hall showed, Frontline Teams run all kinds of programs, especially for children and youth, in the local church, where they work for a year. Oasis team leaders provide members with regular training every Monday in matters such as how to share your faith, how to run youth clubs, and personal spiritual growth. Every member of the team receives support and personal nurture through the team leaders and an Oasis coordinator who visits every team regularly. Team members mature spiritually and local congregations grow.

In 1991, Steven Jack joined a Frontline Team in an Anglican church in a depressed area north of London. The church had a new minister with energy and vision, but only thirty-five people attended, and most were over age fifty. Only four young people came to Sunday school and four to the mid-week club. Working with the pastor, Steven and the other members of his Frontline Team decided to start a vigorous ministry with youth and children. Team members presented programs in local schools and visited playgounds. They soon had twenty-five kids attending their weekly club for ten- to fourteen-year-olds. Their high-profile Halloween party attracted one hundred and ten children. Thirty-five children (ages four- to eleven) started attending a weekly club for kids. Next they started "Just Looking" groups for the parents of the sixty- to sixty-five kids who now came every week to some program at the church. By the end of the year, weekly church attendance was up to sixty to sixty-five. Steven does not suppose that his Frontline Team deserves all the credit. But the team was the catalyst: They provided the arms and the legs for the vision that already existed.

Oasis's Youth Ministry Course is a two-year diploma course. By 1994, thirty-five students were studying in this program that combines the Cambridge Diploma in Religious Studies with practical, hands-on experience in local churches.

Oasis's four-year course on Church Planting and Evangelism is a cooperative program with Spurgeon's College. This fully accredited degree program aims at developing church-planter/evangelists. All Oasis's practical skills in culturally relevant evangelism flow into the training. By developing this program with Oasis, Spurgeon's College and the Baptist Union are making a very significant institutional effort to recover the importance of church-planter evangelists in the life of the church.

Brainstormers is a weekend conference for youth leaders. Jointly sponsored by Oasis, Youth for Christ, and *Alpha* magazine, Brainstormers offers three weekend conferences with workshops on the youth culture and how to develop and run weekly youth clubs. In 1994, twelve hundred people attended Brainstormers events.

Oasis's training programs dramatically transform people's lives. Phyllis was attending a conservative Brethren church in which only men could pray and preach in the congregation. Two weeks in Feet First flabbergasted and then transformed her. She was astounded that after a few days' training, she was out on the street, personally telling people about Jesus. Some accepted Christ. Those two weeks, Phyllis says, "changed my whole outlook on God and that he could use me. I came out from that really fired up."

After that week, she returned briefly to her job of selling ads in newspapers. But that no longer had appeal so she joined a Frontline Team in inner-city London. A number of people became Christians. The next year, she worked with a different Frontline Team in a smaller church without a full-time minister. Phyllis helped lead worship in addition to doing all the usual youth activities. Not a single person came to Christ that year, but Phyllis was not discouraged. In fact she made that church her home congregation after she finished with the Frontline Team, and the church is growing slowly. Today, Phyllis is a full-time Oasis staff member coordinating and pastoring three Frontline Teams in London.

Media. Oasis pays a great deal of attention to how they communicate their message. Their media department is among the best in Christian circles in England today. Other organizations often ask Oasis to promote programs for them.

The church's failure to develop outstanding skills in communication frustrates Steve and his team. "The church," Steve complains, "often thinks it's announcing the message. All it's doing is broadcasting to itself. No one else is listening. The world's gone home to tea, and we're all patting ourselves on the back because we're so correct theologically." Oasis's media department constantly remind themselves and anyone who will listen about studies that show that the verbal part determines only seven percent of the effectiveness of any communication. The rest depends on the vocal and visual elements. So why not get the ninety-three percent right? Oasis asks.

They do! They have become a leader in producing Christian videos. Oasis has also had spectacular success using the secular media. There have been major TV documentaries on Steve and Oasis. Steve appears regularly on GMTV, one of the major British breakfast-TV companies. As a result, GMTV is running an Oasis appeal for money to build a hospital in India.

How does one evaluate Oasis? Oasis has a young team that has accomplished an enormous amount in a short time. Steve reached age thirty-eight in 1994. If God continues to bless and Oasis remains faithful, it will continue to be a wonderful gift to the church in Britain and beyond for a long time to come.

Oasis is pioneering a new kind of mass evangelism. Like Billy Graham, Steve Chalke does city-wide missions. But Steve probably integrates social ministry more completely than any popular evangelist since Charles Finney in the mid-nineteenth century. He also works more closely with local churches and spends more time in training programs than have most popular evangelists. As other younger evangelists adopt what Steve is learning, more and more Christians will understand why Jesus offers both the cup of water and the bread of life.

---

1   Steve Chalke's recollection of the author's statement. Unless otherwise indicated, all quotations are from personal interviews.

2   See Steve Chalke, *The Cracker Manual* (Eastbourne: Kingsway Publications, 1990), for "everything you need to know about running a Christmas Cracker restaurant."

3   This is not her real name.

4   Quoted in Mike Fearon, "Tell Everybody About Him," *Today*, August 1990, 21.

5   I have changed the name.

6   It used to be called Seventy Times Seven.

10
Unleashing the Laity
in a Typical American Church

Without exception, churches that are effective in reaching the unchurched focus on loving people into the kingdom through practical caring.

The Reverend Jimmy Smith

Bear Valley Baptist Church in Denver was a very ordinary congregation. If you had wandered into its modest sanctuary on a Sunday morning in 1970, you would not have sensed anything unusual. It was a small church of about one hundred white middle-class members with an annual budget of less than seventeen thousand dollars. Squeezed in between a church on each side, there was very little space for expansion. And no more interest in change than in a typical contented congregation.

Something unusual, however, began to happen in Bear Valley in the early seventies. Frank Tillapaugh came as pastor and began to preach about unleashing the laity. In fact, he only agreed to come as pastor after the church accepted his request to abolish all standing committees. He did not want his people wasting time on unnecessary church committees inside their ecclesiastical fortress. Instead he urged them to move out into the streets to minister to the poor and broken.

Things began to change. This inward-looking congregation preoccupied with "spiritual" matters began to think about creative outreach ministries. Slowly, one ministry after another started. By 1982, Bear Valley had special ministries for street people, refugees, artists, ex-convicts, mothers of preschoolers, and international students. And the congregation had grown to one thousand. They still worshiped in their small sanctuary that seated about three hundred. Rather than spending money on church construction, they had four separate services each Sunday. And their ministries were scattered all across Denver.

Could other churches do similar things? Tillapaugh is certain the answer is yes. "There is no reason why any church, under the authority of the Scripture, even with very modest facilities, cannot become the home base for a big ministry. First, however, such churches must be convinced that it really can be done. It can be done without new facilities, without moving to the suburbs and without going on TV. These churches possess the nation's greatest, most precious resources. It's not oil or coal; it's people who still live by a value system based on scriptural absolutes. Every Bible-believing church has the rapidly diminishing commodity of people who love, who can be trusted and who have a common commitment to God's revealed absolutes."[1]

How did it happen at Bear Valley? Tillapaugh had a clear vision for the church in the city. First, he rejected the "fortress church" mentality preoccupied with what happens inside the church building. Instead he helped his people see that their real ministry was out in the city wherever people needed help.

Releasing the laity for "front-line" ministry was a central key. When he came to Bear Valley, this little congregation of one hundred people had twenty standing committees. They all disappeared. Direct "front-line" ministry to needy people is far more energizing and important than boring committee meetings about the color of the carpet.

Identifying specific target groups was also important. Tillapaugh helped the congregation view the city in terms of target groups—people with some special shared cultural or social characteristics and needs.

Bear Valley was also careful to build its new programs around people and their sense of call. No matter how intensely church leaders wanted to start some new program, they always waited until lay leadership emerged with enough vision, energy, and skill to raise the funds and lead the program.

Church leaders at Bear Valley longed to see a ministry to singles at Bear Valley, but no layperson sensed the call. For six years, they waited and prayed. Then over a short time, three people came forward, eager to start such a group. Quickly they launched a weekly singles group at a local restaurant. Ministry to singles has been a major program at Bear Valley ever since. "If we have to wait six or seven years for a ministry to begin, that's okay. But when God moves people, our structure must not be in the way."[2]

The next step is to figure out how best to reach the target group. That means going to where they are rather than trying to drag them into the church sanctuary. It also demands responding to their real needs.

Trusting the laity was a central key. Bear Valley's pastors understood their role to be that of equipping the laity for ministry. That did not mean trying to run the programs. The pastors provide encouragement, help with resources, and an annual training conference for all the volunteer "staff" doing frontline ministry, but they trust the laity to raise the funds and operate the programs.

It is hardly surprising that Bear Valley began to grow. During one nine-year period in the '70s, they grew by twenty per cent per year. Their old building was soon bursting at the seams. After some initial struggle, they decided to remodel the old building rather than move to the suburbs and build a new expensive structure. They preferred to spend their money on new ministries. Even the remodeled building could only seat three hundred people, so they added additional worship services. By 1982, there were four—two traditional services with excellent choirs and two more informal alternative services. Occasionally they rented a large auditorium somewhere in the city so all the four congregations could come together for a joint celebration.

Bear Valley believes many churches could do what they have done. "Any church in the city with modest facilities can also grow to many times the number of people they presently serve."[3]

New ministries brought in new people. New people meant more "lay ministers" able to join the front line. One ministry after another began to take shape in various parts of metropolitan Denver.

The story of Bear Valley's ministry to street people shows how they stay open to the moving of the Spirit. In 1977, four couples in the church approached the leadership with an offer. Their small group had just finished reading a book on God and the poor and they wanted to donate six hundred dollars a month beyond their regular giving to start a street ministry. That same week, Tillapaugh's nephew, Andy Cannon, called. He had been working with street kids in Memphis but was ready to come to Denver. They stepped out in faith before they had all the necessary funds and facilities and hired Andy as street pastor. Fortunately, two businessmen donated fifty thousand dollars for a large building that they renamed the Genesis Center, where Andy and his family could live with about thirty people.

Residents followed a careful schedule of meals, Bible study, work crews, and witnessing. Their coffeehouse called "Jesus in Main Street" was a great meeting place. Strict rules on male-female relationships for all residents at Genesis Center brought a desperately needed order and integrity into the chaotic, promiscuous lifestyles of former street kids. Over the first six years, nineteen stable marriages resulted.

In the early '80s, the city rezoned the area, and the Genesis Center became a shopping mall. But Andy's street ministry had been slowly evolving into both a church and a school for high-school dropouts. By 1994, his Open Door Fellowship Church was a thriving congregation of one hundred members. One half of the members are street people and one half are middle-class folk from the suburbs. The Denver Street School has two campuses in Denver and one in Colorado Springs.

The Denver Street School for high-school drop-outs started quickly when a wealthy donor offered to rent a big house for them next door to the Open Door Fellowship. Tom Tillapaugh (Frank's nephew) was a science-and-math teacher who had moved to Denver to work with Andy. They gathered a few high-school drop-outs from the coffeehouse and started a school. "It wouldn't work on paper," Tom says. "It works because the Lord sent fantastic people who would sacrifice their lives for these kids—literally."[4]

Dee Oldham McDonald is one of those committed teachers. After graduating from Colorado State in 1986, Dee faced a very promising future as a gifted African-American professional. She was accepted for study at several law schools. Then in a church bulletin from Bear Valley, Dee happened to see a blurb about the need for teachers at Denver Street School. She has been teaching there ever since.

Today, Denver Street School has forty-five students and a waiting list of one hundred-fifty. Sixty percent of the students are Hispanic, twenty-five percent African-American, and fifteen percent are white. They have eight classrooms, a science lab, a full computer lab, and an auditorium. There is already a second campus in Denver and another in Colorado Springs. Tom has also served as a consultant to help start similar street schools in Seattle and Fort Collins.

Their annual budget of three hundred thousand dollars must come from nongovernmental sources, because Christian faith permeates their programs. Andy Cannon leads daily Bible classes and a weekly chapel. "Bible classes become counseling sessions," Tom says. "We are trying to build character and moral values." Many members from Bear Valley church provide funds and serve as volunteer tutors. The school's basketball and volleyball team use the Bear Valley church's gym as their home court. Links with the Open Door youth group are developing in order to provide a Christian peer group. Tom disagrees with those who say, "Education is the job of the public schools; we just lead people to Jesus." Tom knows his students need "wholistic education— which combines academic, vocational, spiritual, emotional and physical education."

The students at Denver Street School are tough kids from awful homes. Drugs, alcohol, teenage pregnancy, little sense of right and wrong, and hopelessness all haunt their lives. Tom brings in former graduates who have succeeded—to prove that change is possible. Dedicated teachers help these kids develop a moral conscience. Staff become substitute parents, spending not just class time but evenings and weekends with the kids. Tom says, "We tell the kids, 'Jesus loves you and I love you' and they eat it up." In recent years, over half of all the students have accepted Christ. Over half have also gone on to college.

Lisa's[5] boyfriend brought her to the Denver Street School when she was fifteen. Her parents drank heavily, used drugs, and seemed not to care what became of Lisa. So she dropped out of high school and threw herself into drugs and wild parties. She was, Tom explains, "looking for her father's love in her boyfriend's arms." Lisa had one child when she arrived and was pregnant with twins when she left. The intervening years were not easy for anyone. Sometimes bad behavior resulted in expulsion. But two weeks later, she would be back begging to return to the only place where she had found genuine love.

The school became Lisa's family, and she began to change. During her final year, she accepted Christ. She joined the singles group at Bear Valley and discovered a whole different world. Members of the group cared for her children when she enrolled in a computer school after graduation. Today she has a good job. She returned recently to the Denver Street School to share her story. Troubled kids listened intently as this confident, articulate, stylishly dressed young professional told the students how Christ had transformed her life.

Dr. Bob Williams directs the Inner-City Health Center. By 1994, the center was serving over one thousand patients a month in one of Denver's poorest, minority neighborhoods. Nine volunteer doctors and twenty volunteer nurses make possible their modest fee structure with a sliding scale. Staff pray with patients and invite them to church.

The center started as a ministry of Bear Valley. Like a number of other Bear Valley ministries, however, it eventually became independent (in the mid-1980s). But considerable funds and volunteer staff for the center still come from Bear Valley.

Jeff Johnsen is the executive director of an umbrella organization called Mile High Ministries that has emerged to assist several Bear Valley programs. When Jeff moved to Denver in 1982 to play in a country-and-western band, he began to attend Bear Valley. The church's biblical teaching on God's heart for the poor and oppressed was new to Jeff, but he and his band responded when Bear Valley presented the need for sponsors for a Cambodian refugee family. As Jeff struggled to help this family deal with gangs and brokenness in their housing project, "God broke my heart with the concerns and needs of the poor. Sponsoring the family was just a small thing—just about anybody could do it—but it was a hands-on experience. I was feeling their pain and then hearing the pastor say that God wants us to respond."

In the late 1970s, Bear Valley needed a legally independent

umbrella for some of the church's ministries like the coffeehouse, health center, and the ministry to the street people, so the church organized Bear Valley Ministries. Then in 1988, after a Billy Graham crusade helped a number of churches work more closely together, this umbrella agency became fully independent. The senior pastors from ten Denver area churches (including Bear Valley) now form the board of the renamed Mile High Ministries (MHM).

MHM exists to link inner-city and suburban congregations in order to strengthen churches in the inner city. Three of the senior pastors on the board are from the inner city, seven from the suburbs. They meet once a month for half an hour of business and two hours of prayer and worship. Their goal is to provide the resources that will enable strong ministries to emerge in the inner city in order to strengthen local churches there. Jeff, MHM's Executive Director, underlines the central role of the local church: "Nearly one hundred percent of the time if we help people with a particular need, and see them come to know Christ, they almost never continue as a healthy person or disciple unless they are plugged into the local church. The local church is the key indigenous institution for recovering the moral fabric of the community."

MHM is a bridge between suburban and inner-city churches. Predominantly Hispanic Neighborhood Church needs tutors for its educational program, so Jeff recruits them from suburban congregations. In 1990, Andy Cannon's Open Door Fellowship found five abandoned crack houses that he knew could provide just the space they needed to house the congregation's growing ministries. But his inner-city church could not afford the cost of rehabilitation. So MHM raised the money and organized the volunteers and then turned the facilities over to Open Door Fellowship.

That renovation project sparked a new ministry of reconciliation at MHM. As hundreds of mostly white volunteers from suburbs and small towns came in to do renovation in the Hispanic and Black inner city, the leaders at MHM began to sense an opportunity (and need) to use their short stay in the city to nurture a new understanding, so they began to structure their time so that each day the volunteers spent four hours rehabbing buildings and eight hours learning about God's heart for the poor and life in black and Hispanic neighborhoods. Community people welcome the chance to tell white folks "what the real story is in the inner city." Jeff and other MHM leaders have developed a creative program of videos, books, lectures by community people, global-inequities quizzes, and global-hunger games. But nothing hits home more vividly than the evening when the tired, hungry volunteers return for their dinner and are given one dollar in food stamps and told, "Don't come back until 9:00 P.M. Have a nice dinner."

MHM does more than bring in suburban volunteers for short-term work in the inner city. They also have helped about ten families relocate.

Liz and Steve Thompson have been members at Bear Valley since 1986. In fact, Steve was a pastoral intern there while studying at Denver Seminary and later served as full-time youth pastor. Steve took a number of high-school groups on short-term mission trips to Third World countries. Slowly, they and other couples developed a call to move to the inner city. In 1992, they moved to an area next to two other Christian couples, including Dee McDonald and her family. A little later two other couples moved nearby. All six couples have been connected with Bear Valley Church in some way over the years. It's not easy living where they do, although their weekly support group helps. Gunfire from gang warfare often pierces the silence of the night. Liz's and Steve's seven-year-old daughter attends a primarily black Catholic school nearby. But they know God has called them. Liz hopes to become a doctor and work with Dr. Bob Williams at the health center. Steve works part-time at Mile High Ministries as he studies law.

Bear Valley Church has had amazing success at promoting inner-city ministries. But we would have a very distorted picture of Bear Valley if that were all we saw. The church itself has never been located in a poor inner-city neighborhood. Nor did the congregation forget or neglect its core middle-class membership as it nurtured ministries among the poor. "The church unleashed," Frank Tillapaugh insisted all along, "can and should focus much of its ministry on the middle class."[6] Over the years, Bear Valley has sponsored a wide range of such programs—frequent marriage retreats, a thriving singles ministry, mothers of preschoolers, a special program for men, and an outstanding music ministry in the traditional worship services.

Pastor Roger Thompson led a men's group called Tent-makers' Union for many years. Most Christian men, he discovered had no idea how to integrate their faith with their work. Using Acts 18:1–3, Roger helped the men see how they could be active witnesses for Christ in their regular jobs. Roger organized a weekly Wednesday morning group for prayer and encouragement. Twice monthly, men gathered for a 6:15 A.M. breakfast and a lively presentation on some relevant topic.

Susan Kofer started Bear Valley's Mothers of Pre-Schoolers (MOPS) in 1972. For years, MOPS met twice monthly at the church for a full morning. The goal? "MOPS meetings are designed to be a place where young mothers can share, cry, or stomp their feet if need be."[7] With their children playing safely and listening to Bible stories in the nursery, they could relax with crafts, refreshments, and discussion, and listen to a mature woman from the church share her testimony. MOPS meetings have proven to be an excellent place for Christian mothers to bring unchurched friends who in turn have often invited their unchurched friends. Bear Valley has found creative ways to follow up these new friendships with non-Christians in order to attract them to Christ and the church.

By the late 1980s, Bear Valley facilities were bursting at the seams. A congregation of about one thousand was trying to worship in a building that seated about three hundred. Sending some members to help reclaim dying churches helped some, but the Bear Valley "campus churches" that resulted had different preachers and found it difficult to unite around a common vision. Few adult Sunday-school classes met at the church, because the building was overflowing with kids. Christian education was suffering and the church was not growing.

Finally, they merged with a small Baptist church in order to salvage a 3.5-acre suburban property from near-foreclosure. They built nine new facilities, including a sanctuary to seat seven hundred-fifty. They consciously chose to "underbuild" so they would have more people and ministries than available space. By asking regular attendees to park a block away at a junior-high-school's parking lot, they kept people focused on the mission beyond the walls of the church rather than return to some ecclesiastical fortress. To the annoyance of their auditor, they donated two hundred thousand dollars from the sale of one of their satellite church's properties to an inner-city congregation instead of putting it in the building fund for the new facility. In May 1991, they moved to their new church center.

Suddenly, an unanticipated disaster struck Bear Valley. A month after the move, the congregation was shocked to learn that the visionary pastor who had inspired and led them for two decades had fallen into adultery. The pain of betrayal numbed everyone. Frank Tillapaugh confessed to the church and accepted the congregation's discipline. After about a year, the church issued a statement of restoration to the body of Christ. They also said that Frank could not return as their pastor. A weaker congregation would have collapsed, but Bear Valley had successfully unleashed the gifts of its laity. They pulled together and persisted with their wholistic vision. In July 1993, they called a new senior pastor, the Reverend Jimmy Smith, who pledged to carry on the vision. "Without exception," he says, "churches that are effective in reaching the unchurched focus on loving people into the kingdom of God through practical caring."[8]

By 1994, weekly church attendance had grown to about thirteen hundred. And they still have four different worship services each weekend! Every month, ten thousand people stream through the new church building, attending a wide variety of programs for youth, adults, and seniors from both the congregation and the larger community. They sponsor twenty-three different Target Group ministries throughout greater Denver.

Evangelism and social transformation are still both high on Bear Valley's agenda. The church newspaper still promotes wholistic Target Group ministries that are lay-led and self-funding, and informs members on the process for starting new ones. Four new ones started in 1994. Individual members donate a great deal of money and time to the thriving programs in the inner city, described earlier. In addition, the church has a mission's budget of one hundred-seventy-thousand dollars, which helps support forty-two missionary families. Bear Valley is also discovering a fertile field for wholistic ministry to broken people right next door among their suburban neighbors. Responding to the tragedy of family break-up is producing what mission pastor Ed Copps calls "a whole new generation of target groups." People are responding. In 1994, Bear Valley was adding up to thirty new members every month. And a higher percent of these new church members at Bear Valley comes from the conversion of non-Christians than ever before in its history.

Much, to be sure, has changed. The larger facility tends to focus more attention on programs within the church building. The suburban setting leads to a greater emphasis on the problems of middle-class suburbanites. No one has quite the same fervor or fire as Frank did for calling the congregation to pour out their lives for the needy. Only the next decade will tell how much of its old vision Bear Valley will manage to maintain. But in spite of wrenching trauma and sweeping change, their goal is to continue their grand vision and courageous pioneering in ministry to the whole person.

Tony Sturniolo symbolizes the best of Bear Valley. Tony came to Christ a decade ago largely through the personal discipling of Frank Tillapaugh. As he studied the Scriptures, Tony realized that he could not practice law during the week and be a Christian on Sunday. "When you first come to the Lord, you're on fire," Tony says. "I didn't want that fire to go out. The only way to do that was to take it wherever I went, which meant taking it to work."

Tony is a lawyer at Sturniolo and Associates. His specialty is divorce law, but he practices in an unusual way. No matter how strongly the client favors divorce, Tony spends the first part of every session with a client talking about the possibility of restoring the marriage. That is not profitable since he only charges for his legal counsel, not his regular spiritual advice, prayer, and Bible study, so thirty to forty percent of his time is donated. But his main job is helping people reach healing and reconciliation with Christ and spouse.

Four years ago, Tony became so frustrated with the rate of Christian marriages ending in divorce that he founded Marriage

Watchers. The goal is to catch problems before they lead to divorce. Four hundred couples have been in the group in the last four years. One-third to one-half of those have been non-Christians, but prayers and biblical teaching on marriage pervade the monthly meetings.

Tony is also deeply involved in other Bear Valley-related ministries. He has served on the board of the health center and Mile High Ministries. He teaches constitutional law at the Denver Street School. In fact, in June 1994, his firm purchased a building just across the street from the school. Tony wants to be nearby so he can offer legal help to the school and the kids when they need it.

Tony strongly supports Bear Valley's emphasis on "lay ministers." He spends a great amount of time sharing his faith with non-Christians and discipling new believers. "People wear masks on Sunday but take them off during the week," Tony says. That is why he believes that lay ministers like himself have a better opportunity to reach hurting people than do pastors. "Lay ministry," he insists "is the most effective ministry because we're right there. Christians who witness through their lifestyle and in their lives are more effective than anything coming out of the church."

That is what Bear Valley Church is all about.[9]

---

1 Frank R. Tillapaugh, *Unleashing the Church: Getting People Out of the Fortress and Into the Ministry* (Ventura: Regal Books, 1982), 61–62.

2 Ibid., 76.

3 Ibid., 87.

4 Except where otherwise indicated, material in quotations comes from interviews.

5 Not her real name.

6 *Unleashing the Church*, 198.

7 Ibid., 206.

8 Quoted from a church newsletter in April 1994.

9 In 1990, Frank Tillapaugh coauthored *Mastering Outreach and Evangelism* with Calvin Ratz and Myron Augsburger (Portland: Multnomah, 1990).

11
Jesus Action
All Around the Globe

If the Lord had given us great big instructions, we probably would have run the other way. But we felt we were capable of making tea and smiling Jesus-smiles and caring for people.

June Kelsall

How could the people we have met in previous chapters accomplish so much? Are they superheroes and geniuses that come only one or two—or perhaps a dozen or two—each decade? I am certain that is not true. I am fully convinced that God stands ready to accomplish equally powerful things through you and me and literally millions of Christians and tens of thousands of congregations—if we are ready to believe and obey.

What really would that mean? What are the central features of all the ministries we have visited? There are at least eight key elements: (1) unconditional commitment to Christ; (2) a passion for evangelism; (3) a passion for the poor; (4) a concern for the whole person in community; (5) consciously chosen programs to enable committed Christians to develop informal, relaxed friendships with non-Christians; (6) relocation among the needy; (7) partnership with the larger body of Christ; (8) the presence of the Holy Spirit.

The leaders in these stories want to serve Jesus Christ above everything else in the world. They are ready to pay any price and bear any cost that obedient discipleship demands. God called Wayne Gordon as a teenager as he lay in bed promising God that he would do absolutely anything God wanted him to do. That is the indispensable starting point.

From one angle, that kind of commitment sounds hard, almost impossible. The funny thing is that when you do surrender that way, you discover that it is a wonderful way to live. In fact, we have been made to live not only as responsible co-workers but also as obedient servants of the Almighty Creator. So it is hardly astonishing that when we do, we experience both fantastic joy and concrete success.

A passion for evangelism is also crucial. There are thousands and thousands of Christian churches and ministries engaged in meeting people's material needs, but most of them seldom get around to explicitly inviting people to Christ. People do not come to Christ automatically. They come to Christ when the people who serve them also long to share their dearest treasure, Jesus Christ the Savior, and therefore regularly pray for and watch for opportunities to encourage people to believe and obey Him.

That does not mean pushy evangelists. It does not mean insensitively ramming tracts and sermons down people's throats. Friendship evangelism expressed in a genuine concern for the whole person is the preferred way for the people we have visited. But it must be intentional. And it must be a passion for most people in the ministry. As the story of Glen Kehrein and Rock/Circle demonstrates, it is abominably easy to weaken and lose explicit, regular evangelism. It will not happen unless, as at Ichthus Fellowship, the leaders all have an evangelistic heart and then regularly train and encourage their people to do it. It is often easier just to provide lodging or share some food. But unless people are converted, little long-term change occurs.

A passion to empower the poor is also indispensable. All of the ministries we have explored have a special concern for the needy and oppressed. They know that was central to Jesus' announcement of the Good News of the Kingdom (Luke 4:16ff). They preach and practice the biblical truth that we do not truly know God unless we share God's passion for justice for the poor (Jer. 22:16). Whether located in the suburbs or inner city, all the models we have seen devote a central part of their ministry to the weak and marginalized.

Concern for the whole person is another way to talk about much of the previous two features. None of the ministries suppose that they dare care about a person's soul and neglect his body—or vice versa. None of them imagine that the Gospel is merely the forgiveness of sins that one can accept and then go on living the same racist, promiscuous, sinful lifestyle as before. They all know that Jesus' Gospel is the Good News of the Kingdom that transforms believers' relationships with God, neighbor, self, and the earth. They all know that people are not isolated hermits but rather spiritual-physical beings who live in community. Therefore, in obedience to Christ's example and command (John 20:21), they care for the whole person and her surrounding society.

Every ministry described in this book has figured out how to structure relaxed, "non-churchy" settings where Christians with an evangelistic heart can develop informal friendships with non-Christians. The friendships dare not be phony. That is why social ministries that demonstrate practical concern for the whole person are so powerful. Most Christians have few close, ongoing friendships with non-Christians. Growing churches like the ones here have corrected that mistake.

Relocation in some form is also a feature of all the stories. Years ago, John Perkins taught us the importance of the three R's for wholistic mission.[1] The first step, Perkins insisted, is that some people must relocate to the community of need. Vinay and Colleen Samuel moved to the slums of Lingarajapuram. David and Carol Bussau moved to an isolated, devastated village in Bali. The Caseys, Gordons, Kehreins, and Washingtons all moved to inner-city Chicago. Without that costly obedience, their ministries simply would not have happened.

Not everybody must move. All of the stories, in one way or another, involve partnerships between churches with abundant material and technical resources and churches with less. If it is to work, that partnership must be one of mutual dignity, learning, and respect. Financially "poor" churches have much to teach "rich" churches. At the same time, ministries in places like Lawndale, Lingarajapuram, and Sulawesi need outside financial help. If given in a spirit of loving partnership and mutual learning, financial sharing targeted toward nurturing local economic self-sufficiency is essential.

Finally, nothing significant happens without a pervasive, long-term commitment to prayer and dependence on the Holy Spirit. Some of the ministries we have explored are explicitly charismatic, some are not. But a profound sense of reliance on God the Father, Son, and Holy Spirit flows through all of them.

There is a growing sense of the importance of the Holy Spirit among people engaged in wholistic mission. A number of those described in these pages were active in an international dialogue that sought to integrate the three streams of world evangelization, social transformation, and renewal in the power of the Holy Spirit. The final conference in Malaysia in March 1994, issued a Kingdom Manifesto, Kingdom Affirmations, and a Kingdom Prayer that show how all three streams are essential if we want to be faithful to Jesus' whole example.[2]

Fortunately, the number of ministries with a wholistic kingdom vision is growing rapidly. That single fact is one of the most important reasons for being optimistic about the church today. Many other stories could have been included in this book—examples quickly come to mind.

I dedicated this book to John and Vera Mae Perkins because they have pioneered wholistic community development in the United States. John's recent book, *Beyond Charity: the Call to Christian Community Development*,[3] is a powerful inspiration and guide for those who want to learn how to do it. Only about five years ago, Perkins organized the Christian Community Development Association to spread the vision and technical skills for doing what he has done. Five years later, CCDA's annual conference had become a major national event for the American church and membership is increasing rapidly.[4]

I could have talked about Dr. Carolyn Klaus and the wholistic, evangelical health clinic called Esperanza in Philadelphia. Or of Bob Lupton's book, *Return Flight*, that tells the story of relocation to inner-city Atlanta.[5] Or Dr. J. Alfred Smith, Sr.'s marvelous work at Allen Temple in Oakland.[6] Or the Reverend Johnny Ray Youngblood's powerful social ministries and church growth at St. Paul Community Baptist Church in New York City.[7] Or the amazing story of how God has used the Jesus People USA to transform hundreds of lives of drug addicts, alcoholics, and other broken people.[8]

In other continents, too, all around the world, many marvelous examples are emerging. Bishop David Gitari has combined agricultural development, education, and evangelism all across his vast Kenyan diocese and experienced explosive church growth.[9] Malaysian Care's combination of charismatic renewal, miracles, and ministry to drug addicts, prisoners, and the mentally ill has led many to Christ in Kuala Lumpur.[10] The gifts of the Spirit, ministry to the poor, and vigorous evangelism have produced a rapidly growing church at Pablo Deiros' historic Central Baptist Church in Buenos Aires.

The list of wholistic stories is long and growing. More and more of the stories are being told in places like *Transformation*, the international evangelical journal on wholistic mission and ethics.[11] The dramatic pilgrimages described in this book are only a tiny fraction of the successful ministries today truly integrating evangelism and social transformation.

Success stories, however, can intimidate as well as inspire. For many people in a typical church, launching a new Rock/Circle or Bear Valley ministry seems overwhelmingly difficult. Impossible, in fact. One is tempted to despair and do nothing—but that would be to forget a crucial part of the stories we have heard. Every ministry started small. Every ministry experienced struggle and setback.

Just because your congregation cannot do everything now does not mean you should do nothing. Just because you cannot instantly launch all the programs mature ministries now operate after twenty years of struggle does not mean you should not begin with one single program.

Ichthus's Jesus Action would be a simple place for any congregation to start. A small group of folk in any church almost anywhere could gather six to twelve volunteers who agree to volunteer two to three hours a week. Each person would agree to respond to one call for help each week. Then simple postcards or fliers could be posted all around a neighborhood of need near the church: "NEED HELP? Call Jesus Action, 847–2600." No sophisticated training would be needed to get started—just a little encouragement so that each volunteer feels comfortable asking each person at the end of the visit if he or she would like to be prayed for.

It is not hard to see how this kind of simple beginning could grow naturally. The small circle of volunteers will need help. So they will recruit other church members or people from neighboring congregations. They will want a bit of training on how to develop an ongoing friendship so a training program on friendship evangelism[12] can be very helpful. Frequently, volunteers will feel sufficiently overwhelmed that even if regular times for prayer were not part of the original plan (they should have been!), they will soon seem necessary. A prayer ministry to cover every volunteer could easily become a part of the church's small group structure.[13]

As they work daily at tough nitty-gritty issues, they will also want to deepen their biblical, theological foundations for wholistic mission. (That's what my companion volume, *One-Sided Christianity?* offers.)

Some needs will come up again and again. Soon, someone will ask how the church can develop a specific program to meet those recurring needs—for example, a tutoring program, or a housing ministry for the homeless. One thing will lead to another, as the church stays open to the Spirit. After a few years, almost before you realize what has happened, an increasingly comprehensive ministry of evangelism and social transformation will have emerged. Sometimes, as in my own personal case, the whole thing will fail. Sometimes, the efforts will blossom into a Rock/Circle, Lawndale, or Bear Valley.

Often, congregations that want to begin or walk further on the path of integrating evangelism and social transformation will want help from people who are already further down the road. That is exactly what ESA provides for local churches. ESA is an international Christian ministry devoted to helping persons and churches bring together evangelism, social transformation, and spiritual formation. ESA works with local churches, providing initial workshops, tools, material, ideas, and ongoing consultation to help them move toward more wholistic mission. ESA's monthly publication, *PRISM*, shares stories, news, and information about new models and tools.

I am certain God is calling every reader of this book to become involved in some specific way in wholistic ministry. It does not have to be big and complex. It can start with your sharing Jesus' love for the whole person with a couple of needy people you meet this week. The Samuels' vast complex of programs in India started with Colleen sitting under a tree, tutoring a few poor kids. June Kelsall's string of residential homes for abused women in Auckland, New Zealand, started with a couple friends offering a cup of tea and "Jesus smiles" to a few lonely women.[14]

It can be done. You can start now. It may transform you, your church, and your community.

I am convinced that God wants Christians today to develop more and more ministries like the ones described here—hundreds, thousands, tens of thousands all around the world. If we do, God will use the church to change our world in powerful, visible ways.

Changing the world is not really the hard part. Persuading Christians to follow Jesus is the problem. There are almost two billion Christians in the world today. If a mere ten percent of us—that is two hundred million people!—would love and obey Christ the way the people described in this book do, we would see non-Christians converted and societies transformed on a scale never before witnessed in church history. We can hardly begin to imagine what God would do with two hundred million Christians who look into the face of Christ and say with Wayne Gordon: "I want You to know I will do anything that You want me to do with my life."

You and I cannot take that step for the other 199,999,998 million Christians, but we can, by God's grace, pray that prayer for ourselves. I do that again today as I write the final words of this book. I hope you will, too, as you finish reading.

O Lord, please encircle Your world with Jesus Action.

---

1 John M. Perkins, *With Justice for All* (Ventura: Regal, 1982) and *A Quiet Revolution* (Waco: Word, 1976).

2 For these important documents and a Findings Report from the March 1–5, 1994, consultation, see *Transformation*, July-September 1994.

3 Grand Rapids: Baker, 1993. Perkins spent the first ten years of ministry at Mendenhall, Mississippi, and the next ten at Jackson. For information about those ministries written by leaders he trained, see Dolphus Weary and William Hendricks, *I Ain't Comin' Back* (Wheaton: Tyndale, 1993), and Spencer Perkins

and Chris Rice, *More Than Equals: Racial Healing for the Sake of the Gospel* (Downers Grove: InterVarsity, 1993).

4   For CCDA, write to Wayne Gordon, President, CCDA, 3848 W. Ogden Avenue, Chicago, IL 60623 (312–762–0994).

5   Robert D. Lupton, *Return Flight: Community Development through Reneighboring Our Cities* (Atlanta: FCS Urban Ministries, 1993).

6   G. Willis Bennett, *Guidelines for Effective Urban Church Ministry* (Nashville: Broadman, 1983). See also the amazing story of Deliverance Evangelistic Church in North Philadelphia in Lyle Schaller, *Center City Churches* (Abington: 1993), Chapter 5.

7   Samuel G. Freedman, *Upon This Rock: The Miracles of a Black Church* (New York: HarperCollins, 1993).

8   See also Jesus People USA in Chicago and their creative youth publication, *Cornerstone Magazine*, 939 W. Wilson, Chicago, IL 60640 (312–989–2080).

9   See the articles in *Transformation*, October-December 1988, 44–46, and July-September, 1991, 7–17.

10 Betty Young, *Who Cares? The Story of Malaysian Care* (Kuala Lumpur: Malaysian Care, 1991).

11 Since 1988, *Transformation* has published a lengthy series of articles, "Wholistic Models of Evangelism and Social Concern." For back issues and a subscription, write to *Transformation*, 10 Lancaster Avenue, Wynnewood, PA 19096, USA, or to OCMS, P.O. Box 70, Oxford, UK OX2 6HB. Other good recent books on wholistic mission include: David Caes, ed., *Caring for the Least of These: Serving Christ Among the Poor* (Scottdale: Herald Press, 1992); Bruce Bradshaw, *Bridging the Gap: Evangelism, Development and Shalom* (Monrovia: MARC, 1993); and Bryant L. Myers, *The Changing Shape of World Mission* (Monrovia: MARC, 1993). See also James W. Gustafson, "The Integration of Development and Evangelism," *International Journal of Frontier Missions*, October 1991.

12 Joseph Aldrich's *Life-Style Evangelism: Crossing Traditional Boundaries to Reach the Unbelieving World* (Sisters, Oregon: Multnomah, 1983) is a great place to start.

13 Every church needs small groups. A great tool has been written by Michael T. Dibbert and Frank B. Wichern, *Growth Groups: A Key to Christian Fellowship and Spiritual Maturity in the Church* (Grand Rapids: Zondervan, 1985).

14 See Chapter 5.

Bibliography

1. For a number of books on wholistic missions, see the notes to chapter 11 of this book (170–72).

2. For a much larger bibliography, see Ronald J. Sider, *One-Sided Christianity?* (Zondervan/HarperCollins, 1993), 243–50.

3. *PRISM.* This popular monthy magazine is devoted to integrating evangelism, social transformation and renewal in the Spirit, and reviews of materials on wholistic mission. For a subscription, write to: *PRISM*, 10 Lancaster Avenue, Wynnewood, PA 19096. (610) 645-9390.

4. *Transformation.* With readers in sixty-seven countries, this is the only international evangelical journal devoted to wholistic mission and ethics. For a subscription, write to: *Transformation*, 10 Lancaster Avenue, Wynnewood, PA 19096. (610) 645-9390.

Help for Local Congregations

ESA is an organization that helps local congregations who seek assistance in developing more fully their thinking and programs on wholistic mission. Consultation, workshops, materials, and tools to help the local congregation integrate evangelism and social transformation are available. Write ESA, 10 Lancaster Avenue, Wynnewood, PA 19096. (610) 649-8090.

Persons interested in further information about meetings, programs, and materials that seek to implement this book's call for wholistic mission that combines evangelism and social action, are invited to write to:

Ron Sider, President
Evangelicals for Social Action
10 Lancaster Avenue
Wynnewood, PA 19096
Phone: 610-645-9390
Fax: 610-649-8090